The Philosophy of Marx

LA FILOSOFIA DI MARX

— THE PHILOSOPHY OF MARX —

GIOVANNI GENTILE

Translated by
Shandon Simpson and Caterina Vitale

ANTELOPE HILL PUBLISHING

First printing 2022.

Originally published in Italian as *La filosofia di Marx* by Pisa: Enrico Spoerri, 1899. This translation is of the 1937 edition, which differs from the original 1899 edition only by the addition of a note by Gentile.

English translation by Shandon Simpson and Caterina Vitale, 2022.

Where English translations exist for cited works, those editions are given along with the wording from those translations. Otherwise, quotations from the original given in Italian have been translated into English by Simpson and Vitale with the citation matching that of the original book. Some citations were not given in the original for smaller quotations, and a portion of those remain uncited in this edition.

Cover art by Swifty.
Edited by Caterina Vitale and Margaret Bauer.
Formatted by Margaret Bauer.

Antelope Hill Publishing
www.antelopehillpublishing.com

Paperback ISBN-13: 978-1-956887-08-2
EPUB ISBN-13: 978-1-956887-09-9

"It was Gentile who prepared the road for those—like me—who wished to take it."

Benito Mussolini

As quoted in *The Ideology of Fascism: The Rationale of Totalitarianism,* by A. James Gregor

Contents

Preface to the Original 1899 Edition

Here I collect two critical studies on the often criticized philosophy of Karl Marx, which today is passionately discussed by followers and opponents alike without any hope of agreement on the philosophy's special doctrines or overall strategy. Was he a materialist, or not? Which doctrine is closest to that fortunate type of historical materialism popularized around the world by Marx? Which is closest to his revolutionary idea? Is there really a relation between this historical materialism and metaphysical materialism, in the strictest sense of the word?

In the first of the two studies,[1] I analyze and criticize historical materialism (or at least what Marx meant by historical materialism) as a theory of history—I did not attempt to search for which philosophy was inherent to the theory. On the contrary, I wrote that Marx's "historical materialism is no place to pose questions concerning spiritualism and materialism." Additionally, I agreed with Croce's position that the self-supplied influences of historical materialism should be considered unreliable. I also refrained from denying that Marx and Engels were materialists, regardless of whether their theory of history could be described as such. I instead concluded that they, as materialists and followers of the "philosophical movement, meant as a reaction to idealism, started by the Hegelian Left and continued by Moleschott, Vogt, and Büchner," could have thought of their reaction to Hegel's philosophy

---

1 First published in *Studi storici*, ed. Amedeo Crivellucci, Vol. 6 (Pisa: 1897), 379–423.

as materialistic by simple analogy! In my second study, I examine and analyze the philosophy of Marx as metaphysical materialism. Have I therefore changed my opinion?

Truly, no. It will be helpful to explain how and why my second study has not obliged me to change the thoughts expressed in the first study in the slightest, and which I will now repeat here with only faint stylistic revisions.

Yes, there is a metaphysical materialism in Marx that defines itself as historical materialism. But was his theory of history born from the depths of metaphysics? Or was the metaphysics devised to provide a philosophical justification for his theory? My analysis of Marx's metaphysical materialism confirms to me that his theory didn't naturally develop from his philosophy, but that the philosophy was artificially concocted to allow Marx (and Engels as well) to take a philosophical position after developing his revolutionary doctrine in Brussels in 1845. His revolutionary economic and historical ideas, published in the French-German Annals in Paris in 1844 in collaboration with Arnold Ruge, had already started to develop when he and Engels began pivoting to philosophy. In fact, in the June 28th, 1883 preface to *The Communist Manifesto*, Engels clearly states that:

The basic idea of this manifesto: that economic production, and its determinant effect on the structure of society in every historical period, is the basis for the political history of that period; that accordingly (since the end of prehistoric communal ownership of land), the entirety of history has been about class struggle, about exploited and exploiting classes, and about dominated and dominating classes at various degrees of social development; that this struggle has now reached a stage where the oppressed and exploited class (the proletariat) cannot free itself from the oppressive and exploiting class (the bourgeoisie) without simultaneously permanently freeing the entirety of society from oppression and exploitation—this basic idea [which is the theory of history that I criticize in my first study] belongs entirely and exclusively to Marx.[2]

He also adds in a footnote:

This concept—which, in my opinion, is certain to cause within the discipline of history a shift equal to that which Darwin's theories effected in the natural sciences—is something that both Marx and I had been independently developing for several years prior to 1845. This is demonstrated well enough in my book, The Condition of the Working Class in England. But when I met Marx in Brussels in 1845, he had already developed it and expressed it to me just as clearly as I express it here now.[3]

Since historical materialism wasn't developed as a metaphysical system until 1845–46,[4] then clearly the revolutionary theory of history had been created before, and independent of, the metaphysical system of critical communism. The critique that this metaphysical system will be subject to in my second study will easily show the efforts taken to justify the claim that the socialistic doctrine was founded on materialist philosophy, which in itself is truly a contradiction of terms.

Thus, historical materialism can be contemplated in two ways: as a theory of history, whose principles can be summarized by Engels' abovementioned description of the basic idea of the *Manifesto*—and as such represents an insight into Marx's thinking; and as a metaphysics or worldview, based on the contrived construction that Marx designed in 1845–46 and applied so as to take a philosophical stance—in essence this

---

2 From the 1883 German edition. This and all other quotations cited from non-English sources were translated by Zoltanous and Caterina Vitale.
3 Karl Marx and Friedrich Engels, *Il manifesto del Partito comunista* (Milano:1896), 8.
4 See § III on the second study.

represents an additional development of Marx's thinking to a degree on which Marx himself didn't insist. It was, in fact, a grotesque overdevelopment of his thinking. In any case, these two elements of Marxist theory are separately studied in the two following parts of this work. The second part demonstrates something that is fleetingly implied in a note in the first part: that a false analogy made by Marx (and Engels) led him to believe that his economic understanding of history was in some way connected to materialism.

All of Karl Marx's philosophical thinking—as vague, fragmented, and lacking in any kind of scientific rigor as it was—is here exposed to an accurate analysis and a new critique, which could perhaps assist the theorists of communism to deal a little bit better with philosophy in the future.[5]

Giovanni Gentile
Campobasso, February 20th, 1899

---

5 It was permitted, in the volume of 1899 in which I gathered these studies, to have the following dedication to Benedetto Croce, which is reported here as a document of the past, connected to these studies:

My Dear Friend,

I wish that this pamphlet—of which you know the origins and in which you'll find many ideas that we have formerly discussed together in our frequent debates—were dedicated to you, as a sign of gratitude for the cordial thoughtfulness you often have towards my poor studies, and as a written declaration of the immense esteem I have of your intellect and character.

From the number of times your name can be found in these pages, you'll be able to deduce how much my spirit is gratified by conversing with yours. In fact, I admire your joyous union of speculative faculties with historical ones, of the need of principles to live with facts, with that of facts uniting and building an ideal organism, because it's an extremely rare type of realism in Italy—so easy to preach and so hard to comprehend—from which I believe my thoughts do not differ much.

However, I'll often quote you to contradict you; and more than once, perhaps, our opinions oppose. But hopefully it won't go unnoticed to the clever reader, nor to you, that our fundamental judgement on the philosophy I criticize in this pamphlet is identical.

After all, you also won't doubt for a moment that our disagreements on these scientific researches could ever be the cause of the decrease of the affection your friend has for you etc.

G. G.
Rome, January 3rd, 1937

Note from the 1937 Edition

In this volume,[6] I've reprinted an early work of mine from almost forty years ago (*La Filosofia di Marx,* in *Studi critici,* Pisa: Spoerri, 1899) at the insistence of scholars who sought it—especially after they discovered that even Lenin had read my pamphlet and had regarded it as one of the most noteworthy studies done by a non-Marxist on Marx.[7] I'll also say that while I have avoided republishing it for two or three decades because of a vague memory of the essay having some faults, and while it is dated because of all of the new studies that have come to light and because of the release of new documents regarding Marx's thinking to scholars, I've convinced myself to read this old, forgotten essay once again. I reread it with the nostalgic curiosity that we occasionally experience when looking through our old papers to revive faded memories and images from our distant youth. As I read I heard once again, here and there, voices that have never died out in me, recognized in myself some fundamental things, and saw other things that perhaps others more intellectual than myself would be able to recognize as the first seeds of thoughts that later matured.

Therefore I have recognized in my book, despite its dated content, a historical value that has made me find life again where I feared death had come forever.

---

6 In his 1937 reprint of this work as an appendix to "The Foundations of the Philosophy of Law," Gentile began with an admonitory preface from which the part regarding the studies of Marx is reproduced here.

7 Vladimir Lenin, "Karl Marx." In *Granat Encyclopedic Dictionary,* 7th ed., 1915.

For this reason, I approved the republication, but left the book as it was, with all of its faults, neither adding nor erasing anything. I sought to avoid creating something new that both was and was not the previous text, deprived of documentary value for matters first pondered at the end of the last century—a time in Italy when myself and others began to feel the need to help build a true kind of philosophy.

I therefore limited myself to simple adjustments of form, preserving many traces of abstruseness and juvenile uncertainty.

Giovanni Gentile
Rome, January 7th, 1937

— A CRITIQUE OF HISTORICAL MATERIALISM —

I.

Contemporary Importance of Socialistic Studies

To some people, the great scientific advancements today pertain to social matters, and though such issues are indeed debated in every age and are never quite out of sight, recent developments reflect the distinct character of our times. I think it's appropriate to show how excessive this statement is from the start; first and foremost, by making a precise and important distinction in the matter that we're going to discuss.

It is true that a great clamor is rising everywhere, and perhaps not without reason it can be said that each day it more loudly proclaims this preeminence; affirming that the research of social problems is and must be the special task of our age, mature or approaching maturity, to finally start finding the definitive solution to a matter as old as Man's consciousness, that is as old as the whole of Man's history.

However, even those who study the historical moment we're going through, are studying it with the calm critique of science, and they are not left stunned by clamorous statements. They draw aside, where the rash screaming can't go so far as to disturb their judgment, and instead they concentrate on the actual state and reason of things, rather than on the multitude that follows this scream down a long road, as it caresses great hopes and raises infinite desires.

And actually, the supporters of that preeminence don't give as much attention to the authority and the results of the research produced around purported social matters as they do to the great crowd of those that discuss it and converse about it on a daily basis—in newspapers and books—or to how many people are right to take interest in it (and far from being too few, there are unfortunately too many of these!). But alas, if every science had to take into account the solutions—perhaps sometimes novel ones, and nevertheless always certain!—that have been devised by the crowd that often takes part in such discussions! Surely the annals of every discipline would gain much in the extent and number of volumes that could be written; but perhaps some other parts would be lost. And think of the grave risk that would be taken if we were to really listen to the demands of anyone who offers a historical evaluation of the cultural movement we still live in, without making a distinction between what has a scientific character and what doesn't. In so doing, we'd lose the beneficial perspective that posterity will have, falling easily into error. Genuine scholarship would get mistaken for improvised chatter, at times even for the unsettled fidgeting of political parties; all of which may be of great political significance, but it surely does not have anything to do with science.

Science certainly can and should report the real conditions of society, but it must not and indeed cannot mix them up and make them into something set apart from what their essential nature consists of. This essence is the actual product of the spirit's formal elaboration, for which the conditions of society are destined to provide the basic matter. And, together with the practical distress, all of the endless literary production that is thrown together day by day in that field of study belongs to the content or the matter of science, even though it never brings a new concept or view. Thus, it has weight only for the conscious purpose of disclosure and propaganda: namely, it serves to demonstrate the constantly rising interest in social issues, albeit without suggesting it. In this second case too, it is a sign of a non-proper science. It's an obvious distinction; but it never seems to have been so difficult to observe, and as important as it is today, to appreciate the range of studies that arise from contemporary socialism.

Because if, for the second half of the century, the branch of social sciences gathered under the title of sociology has represented the need to build a historical reality in a logical and scientifically intelligible system (although in an inadequate and philosophically incorrect form), towards which the greatest interest of the mindset of idealistic speculation in the first decades of this century has oriented itself; then it wouldn't be easy to point out the construct of political and social doctrines that have proliferated around socialist movements, and those that tend to philosophize, in the history of the scientific or speculative spirit. Great faith, great dogmatism, scarce critique and arbitrary methods. Bold perspectives about the future, built upon faltering fundamentals of a history that has been fabricated more than it has been studied, examined and understood. Piddling and debatable slapdash observations on economy, and a casual mix of general concepts taken here and there from current philosophies: all of it blended in a rudely pretentious doctrine, baptized with the German taste for coining pretentious scientific-sounding names. This is the substance of socialistic literature, over which professional scholars waver between disdainful *odi profanum vulgus* and the particular embarrassment of those who have not done their homework.

However, when we talk about socialistic studies in particular, as we attempt to, or as we think we are able to, speculatively reconnect their origin with the idealistic transformation that made the cult of history flourish again, then we see that they haven't brought forward a great deal of achievements or even any genuine scientific findings. Indeed, it is not right to consider their theories about the future as though they were the Reason of tomorrow, while disagreement lingers *sub judice* regarding their assertions about the past. What is asserted about the past with the intent and pretension of a scientific theory surely wouldn't be insignificant, if it were based on unconditional principles and proceeded with a truly critical method; but the copious socialist literature is supported by neither a firmness of principles, nor an awareness of the demands of a sane scientific method.

It is necessary, then, to apply *unicuique suum* and to avoid the exaggeration of the reach of these studies. We must not give them a greater value that what they actually possess, and which many of us still refuse to recognize in them. Certainly in Germany, France and England, philosophy has for some time been seriously concerned with these matters, which we here have left to sectarian discussions or to the superficial judgement of the philosophers of particular sciences. They have been casually debated by the best philosophers, but, most often, they've been dragged out by newspapers and pulp fictions aimed at the easy approval of the most willingly pleased public. The consequence of this general neglect from the only people who would be able to measure the theoretical value of certain doctrines (which, blindly taken, manage to create in the most stable beliefs and the strongest resolution) could be easily imagined, if only it weren't being demonstrated all around us every day.

Such a sweeping change of the whole social structure in which we now live is a consequence of a gradual shift; that has never been interrupted since we started living as a society, that is to say for as long as we could be called mankind. And since, as proven by sociology and expressed by philosophy, there aren't and there cannot be people without ethical bonds, lacking family and estate—such a structure cannot support itself for long, without being sustained by a radical new revelation on life and history; that is, without it taking inspiration from a new philosophy. It's a fact proven by the history of socialism that generally the ideal settlement of any utopian society relates to itself (either conspicuously or not) via a special philosophical route or system; so that it would be the same to remove the philosophical fundamentals from which the utopia is born, as to unmask the selfsame utopia; so we must expect that it could find its anchorage in philosophy, stating it, fully maturing its own relations with the philosophical ideas cited, to accurately examine the titles that it has presented to be received into the fair field of science.

Now it looks as though the most recent socialistic form—which occupies the field undisputed, and which received an early boost from the thoughts and actions of Karl Marx and is therefore tied to his name and is properly called *critical communism*—has definitively formulated its theoretical doctrine. This theoretical doctrine is such that, were it to be demonstrated with evidence, it would make any debate on the many matters argued regarding socialism useless.

This doctrine consists in the so-called materialist conception of history; through which, with a firm critique, one could determine a stable and necessary trend over the course of human events, so as to allow the further development of social forms.

II.

The Matter of a Materialistic Conception of History

Among the many issues, constantly raised and rekindled in social literature by the theoretical premises of socialism in recent years, there may be one that is the most debated and undefined, upon which not even the most scholarly and influential socialists have been able to reach agreement. People are investigating whether this concept accords the new doctrine a place in the history of philosophy, in the strictest sense of the word. And if it does, what relation does it have with the philosophical systems from which it was born or to which it gives rise?

By claiming to be a disciple of Georg Hegel, Karl Marx, author of this doctrine, has thereby admitted that he is pleased to flirt (*kokettieren*) with the dangerous terminology of his master. But, was it just about words? His friend and colleague Friedrich Engels, in a characteristic paper exploring the dependence of historical materialism (the soul and core of critical communism) on that system from which it appears and is said to be most directly related, admitted the existence of a strong connection to the degenerated Left Hegelians, particularly with Feuerbach's Hegelianism, the farthest from the master's spirit and principles. [8]

So was the matter exhausted, such that there would be nothing left to say about it? On the contrary, as if invited by Marx's declarations, there has been no shortage of people striving in every way to connect historical

---

8 See Friedrich Engels, *Feuerbach: The Roots of the Socialist Philosophy*, trans. Austin Lewis (Chicago: Charles H. Kerr & Company, 1903).

materialism with the philosophy of Hegel, principally attempting to clarify the relation between the antithetical content and the analogous form, as has been demonstrated by the author in *Das Kapital (Capital)*; and there have been people who have judged Marxism to be a true implementation of Hegelianism, and people who have resolutely criticized any mutual relevance, by only recognizing a mere shared vocabulary that needn't be overly scrutinized. Meanwhile, while conversing on the nature and the form of the doctrine to establish its historical genesis, everyone has wandered around the subject so much that at this point the burdened problem is now more undefined than ever; and one also finds the very appellation of "historical materialism" to be incorrect, as it is by all means unjustified and a producer of misunderstandings. Hence the debate is still lively; the scholar of the history of philosophy cannot lose interest in it.

And among our people, professor Alessandro Chiappelli, one of the most diligent enthusiasts of the history of philosophy and a vigilant examiner of movements in modern thought, has engaged in it for some time with his usual breadth of information, through a series of articles.[9] Recently, he debated the matter in a long essay printed among the proceedings of the Academy of Moral and Political Sciences, Naples— since he belongs to the Spaventa family—to present research of a speculative nature.[10] I must mention also Benedetto Croce, who has made many ingenious and suitable observations around historical materialism. In a brief but rich essay, read in May 1896 at the Accademia Pontaniana, he delicately remarked that perhaps it would be appropriate to consider again, once and for all, these self-professed relations between scientific socialism and Hegelianism, with precision and critique.

---

9 See Alessandro Chiappelli, *Il Socialismo e il pensiero moderno*, (Firenze: Le Monnier, 1897).

10 *Le premesse filosofiche del socialism*, 1897.

The expository literature of historical materialism is also plentiful, if we consider how it has only been distinctly formulated and connected to the contemporary socialist movement in recent times.

It's a new visual angle from which to look at history. A new method and a new system, from which is announced that we will have to start all over again to explain the human facts; a new understanding of life, and, in a word, a new philosophy. It is not yet intended to set up, gradually and as a result of progressive transformation of the content and character of the national or generational culture, new modes of civilization and of daily life. Nevertheless it is already a tool and a theoretical interpretation concurrent with a social revolution, not platonically referring to a possible or probable condition to take place, but now resolutely underway with enthusiasm and faith. This is what the new doctrine demands to be. It's no surprise that it has drawn the attention of many, advocates and opponents alike, who seek to build up and direct the fundamental ideas of the early authors, in order to reduce the new thinking to a consistent unity. And just as in the intertwining of social movements, the one spearheaded by Marx has gradually taken over any other form of socialism, and it has gathered almost every effort of the social class that arises against the present set of rules and summed them up within itself, just as new life-giving blows to the theoretical dissertation of the doctrine have come from the same practical foundation.

Fervet opus in Germany; but in Italy so far we have had two important displays and dissertations on the materialistic theory of history thanks to professors Achille Loria and Antonio Labriola. Notwithstanding, the former (who isn't a socialist) is not strictly speaking an interpreter of Marx's thinking, and, while trying to elaborate the concept of the economical foundations of the social establishment on his own, he has moved away from Marxism and has exposed himself to severe but fair criticism from those willing to recognize the gravity of Marx's concepts.[11] On the contrary, professor Labriola is undoubtedly the most competent one among those who have embraced this faith and this social science in Italy, and he has dedicated assiduous studies for many years to illustrate the doctrine of historical materialism in his most genuine and accomplished style.[12] That is to say, within the ideal proposed by Marx and which can be logically developed, according to the general views and the intention and the particular applications of the master, with respect to the different problems of philosophy, law and politics. For now, it has given rise to two essays, firstly to expose the genetic development of the new historical doctrine and the rationale for it as expressed within the classical document of Marxist socialism that is the *Manifesto*, published by Marx and Engels in London in February 1848, at the eve of the revolutions in Europe. Secondly, to disentangle from its various aspects and define this doctrine with scientific prudence, examining and establishing the original meaning, determining its range, and especially getting himself to trim down every error of interpretation and of exaggeration, whence the inexperienced have overdone it. Yet we believe it appropriate to portray, from these very recent books of this talented professor from Rome, the key elements of the new historical conception, which we intend to evaluate in relation to philosophy.

---

11 See Benedetto Croce, *Le teorie storiche del prof. Loria* (Napoli: Giannini, 1897). Much of this work has been reproduced in English in Benedetto Croce, *Historical Materialism and the Economics of Karl Marx*, trans. C.M. Meredith (New York: The Macmillan Company, 1914).
12 See Antonio Labriola, *Essays on the Materialistic Conception of History*, trans. Charles H. Kerr (Chicago: Charles H. Kerr & Company: 1908).

III.

Presentation of the Materialistic Conception of History

It has been said that the doctrine of historical materialism was first enunciated, with clear and sharp awareness, in the *Manifesto* of 1848, thrown to the workmen and all the proletarians of the world by Karl Marx and Friedrich Engels. But the true author of it, certified by Engels himself, is Marx, who had formerly matured the generating concept, and then developed it more deeply.

In the preface of a book that is rightly said to be the prelude to *Capital*, entitled *A Contribution to the Critique of Political Economy*, Marx summarizes his reflections on the pace of history, in a passage that by now is widely cited and which is still useful to report:

In the social production which men carry on they enter into definite relations that are indispensable and independent of their will; these relations of production correspond to a definite stage of development of their material powers of production. The sum total of these relations of production constitutes the economic structure of society—the real foundation, on which rise legal and political superstructures and to which correspond definite forms of social consciousness. The mode of production in material life determines the general character of the social, political and spiritual processes of life. It is not the consciousness of men that determines their existence, but, on the contrary, their social existence determines their consciousness. At a certain stage of their development, the material forces of production in society come in conflict with the existing relations of production, or—what is but a legal expression for the same thing—with the property relations within which they had been at work before. From forms of development of the forces of production these relations turn into their fetters. Then comes the period of social revolution. With the change of the economic foundation the entire immense superstructure is more or less rapidly transformed. In considering such transformations the distinction should always be made between the material transformation of the economic conditions of production which can be determined with the precision of natural science, and the legal, political, religious, aesthetic or philosophic—in short ideological forms in which men become conscious of this conflict and fight it out. Just as our opinion of an individual is not based on what he thinks of himself, so can we not judge of such a period of transformation by its own consciousness; on the contrary, this consciousness must rather be explained from the contradictions of material life, from the existing conflict between the social forces of production and the relations of production. No social order ever disappears before all the productive forces, for which there is room in it, have been developed; and new higher relations of production never appear before the material conditions of their existence have matured in the womb of the old society. Therefore, mankind always takes up only such problems as it can solve; since, looking at the matter more closely, we will always find that the problem itself arises only when the material conditions necessary for its solution already exist or are at least in the process of formation. In broad outlines we can designate the Asiatic, the ancient, the feudal, and the modern bourgeois methods of production as so many epochs in the progress of the economic formation of society. The bourgeois relations of production are the last antagonistic form of the social process of production—antagonistic not in the sense of individual antagonism, but of one arising from conditions surrounding the life of individuals in society; at the same time the productive forces developing in the womb of bourgeois society create the material conditions for the solution of that antagonism. This social formation constitutes, therefore, the closing chapter of the prehistoric stage of human society.[13]

Here is all of Marx's thinking and work; here, in its native form, in a short formula and like a seed, is every part of the materialistic theory of history and the authentic source of any determination that the best interpreters give.

Now, in the quoted passage there's a sentence which is particularly remarkable and full of meaning, and which actually contains the philosophical concept of everything else: "*It is not the consciousness of men that determines their existence, but, on the contrary, their social existence determines their consciousness.*" Where *man* is not to be interpreted as the human being in his natural state, as the French philosophers of the eighteenth century understood it; but as the social man, the historical man, already equipped with all of the *ideologies*; and *social being* is to be explained as the conditions among which and for which life must perform in a given society; the conditions are neither political, religious, moral, scientific nor artistic, they are simply and solely economical; since these are the creators of all of the other particular forms.

The political, religious, moral, scientific, and artistic conditions or formations are further structures of the man that has already entered society, meaning when he's definitively emerged from prehistory; and this logical and chronological priority, which happens in the early

---

13 Karl Marx, *A Contribution to the Critique of Political Economy*, trans. N.I. Stone (Chicago: Charles H. Kerr & Company, 1859), 11–13.

development of human coexistence, repeats itself regularly any time the social order renews itself, due to some internal revolution.

Therefore, such conditions or structures appear when man has already established his material amenities in a certain way with other individuals of society; and in the new creations derived from the application of his activities to the needs of life in which he gradually gets satisfaction, he *naturally* can neither avoid the influence of this first foundation, nor he can act or move outside of the *artificial field*, as Labriola calls it, in which he has found himself as he came out of prehistory. Hence, he can neither freely give himself a political model, nor a religion, morals, produce any science, any art. He must accept them, or even better, he must produce them just if they are appropriate, and they can only be appropriate in that first form, which is like second nature, and which has necessarily had to accommodate or, more precisely, to produce to solve the first natural needs of its existence. The building of its history cannot be elevated but on the foundation that he's found himself laying. This higher building, this whole of additional historical forms of social life, makes up the complex or the organism of *ideologies* for communism; where the foundations (in which it is the first condition of society) would be its economic structure, the natural basis of all of history.

Thus, it is not by connecting with the erudite study of the mutual relations of different ideologies, that we retrace history or explain its origin and state its ultimate motive. Look into any complex fact of history. It'll appear to you as a complicated arrangement, which you'll unravel to understand it, resorting to analysis, and you'll take it apart in multiple and different elements; then you'll try to reconnect these elements under certain performed ideological categories; which, in the end, will put the keys of mystery in your own hands, indicating the more or less remote causes, containing the fundamental explanation of the fact that you'd wanted to rebuild and make comprehensible.

But in the meantime, you won't have made anything more than a deceiving tautology; you will have stayed in the surface, and, believing to have found the inspected cause, you will have settled for simply trading a fact with another fact, an effect with another effect, not even having suspected its communal cause.

The news couldn't be more important. The recent doctrine has made us aware of a serious illusion, to which our historical sense has always been subject; it demonstrates that the most powerful efforts made by the human spirit so far to understand itself, just like it has been done with history, are all unconsciously useless, so we have to go back where we started and give up all the science we had already achieved. A new visual angle, says Labriola; but much more different from those that we have been adopting for the historical study, that history appears as completely changed from this visual angle.

It's actually an overturning. Marx ironically observed that Hegel puts history on the head; we have to turn it upside down and put it back on the feet. This sentence—that declares the realistic purpose of Marx, while it stings or wants to sting (we'll see that it doesn't even touch it) the prior dialectic construction, that the great philosopher from Stuttgart made of history with his utmost idealism—shows the option in which the new doctrine wants to locate itself toward Hegelianism. History was idealized in this, while it was objectified in materialism, as Labriola says, it was naturalized; in the one First and Immanent in history was the Idea; in the other is, or it is believed to be, the opposite principle, but also its natural fundament, matter. Matter, well intended in a relative meaning, as a social substrate of any ideology.

As Labriola conveniently notices, in terms of *naturalizing* history, a very dangerous ambush is hidden: "a great seduction," he says, for the hasty theorists of socialism. At this point, we like to notice that it looks like he remembers the idealistic origins of critical communism. And rightly so; because in times like this, of proud scientific charlatans, where all the ideas in vogue do all they can for the christening of science, while

the latter condones a single order of elaborations of the human spirit—
those referring to the study of nature or that can be coordinated to it—
it's never enough to notice the great distinction that creates the
appearance of the mentality, or the principle, as Labriola would say, "of
the historical human becoming and living," in the facts that are offered
to the study of man.

In Italy, a great study has been made to ally socialism with the so-
called positive science, meaning, with this incorrect denomination,
Darwinism or the naturalistic Evolutionism. The reason for this attentive
justification—since it a justification, in the eyes of those who have
studied it—is obvious. The desire for a union of poorly intended science
and even more poorly devised; and since this sacred word of "evolution"
now has to be employed for everything if we yearn for the respect or the
consideration of certain philosophers, even the communist State (a most
recent term and a consequence of the social movement) must come from
a series of pre-ordered transformations, for that purpose. We also forget
that if we shifted the battle for existence and the natural selection, which
are principles that lead to Darwinism, from the natural and pre-human
world (which is the one they belong to) to the historical human world,
they would lead to a totally different social development, without a doubt,
that communists do not want.

It's the revolution, not the evolution, that invokes the astute critical
communism of Marx; because it's by solving and destroying the
antithesis that we solve an antithetic state or a social contradiction,
instead of transforming it—when it is possible to do so! And against the
followers of the so-called *political and social Darwinism* Labriola, with
great intellect, observes this:

A certain social life with customs and institutions, even if it be of
the most elementary form that we know, that is to say, of the
Australian tribes, divided into classes and practicing the marriage

of all the men of one class with all the women of another class,
separates human life by a great interval from animal life.[14]

And it does so, as we say, for that *a priori* ethic typical of man, that sociology—great enemy of *a priori!*—has failed to deny.

Labriola accepts the deep view of Vico, about history being made by people—perhaps a much deeper view than Karl Marx had thought, taking it from Ludwig Feuerbach. And, on behalf of his doctrine, he avoids any alliance with the science of the unconscious and fatal animal transformations of the inferior nature. We're dealing with something else here: man doesn't move around nature anymore, but in an artificial environment, that is, in a new world that he has created, distinguishing himself from any other species. He has essentially modified the natural conditions and has made his own, which, as we've seen, will regulate all of history, remaining as a necessary foundation of it. The new task of "naturalizing" history consists in recognizing the incessant efficacy of that on this; since, this way, we can omit "all the ideological views which, in the interpretation of history, start from this hypothesis, that human work or activity are one and the same with free will, free choice and voluntary designs."[15] However, we've come to recognize a necessary and immanent method in history.

---

14 Labriola, *Essays*, 116.
15 Ibid., 121.

IV.

Is the Materialistic Idea a Philosophy of History?

A necessary and immanent method in history. There is, then, a type of science that determines the law of the method—there is a philosophy of history. Is historical materialism a philosophy of history, or should it be? This is a thorny matter, in which opinions are at odds, but to which no one has dedicated a critical discussion; even though it deals with the true essence of the historical doctrine of critical communism and, when determined negatively, it could seriously undermine the theoretical beliefs of socialists.

Actually, Labriola considers the historical materialism as "the ultimate and definitive philosophy of history." But Croce observes that the originality of it is, indeed, of having given up any claim of establish the law of history, of finding the concept to which the complex historical facts are reduced. There's the belief "better homage would be rendered to the materialistic view of history, not by calling it *the final and definite philosophy of history* but rather by declaring that properly speaking *it is not a philosophy of history*."[16] But then, what is the value of the new conception, if it isn't a philosophy of history? Here lies the true fact of the matter.

Chiappelli hesitates, and fails to find a precise definition. In the past, recalling Labriola's second essay, he stated—perhaps not very precisely— that he "doesn't want it to be about a historical philosophy, but rather

---

16 Croce, *Historical Materialism*, 11.

about a methodological view and a critique of history." Nevertheless, he adds, "but what is it, if not a universal conception of this?" Then he calls it "a new philosophy of history (I'm not sure if it's definitive), although it's extremely different from the old technological and metaphysical constructions, which imagined to sum up the whole course in a single view and include the meaning in a single law;" he also remembers that Engels too thought that the historical materialism wasn't a true philosophy of history anymore. But it is certain that in the analysis that he makes of the new doctrine in relation to Hegel's historical philosophy, and in the formal analogy that he acknowledges, he shows how he considers the historical materialism as a true philosophy of history, which, in fact, he states very frequently.

Of course, we must examine if materialism could really be the theoretical expression of critical communism, since, as Croce claims, it isn't a philosophy of history, and if it's right to agree with Labriola that the scientific socialism enunciates "the coming of communistic production, not as a postulate, nor as the aim of a free volition, but as the result of the *processus* immanent in history."[17]

This is what Labriola says about it, who we often come back to, because, by being loyal to Marxism he's felt the theoretical demands, thanks to the philosophical inclination of his mind, and he's managed to examine the speculative consequences of the principles of Marxism and their scientific value:

> *The historic forecast which is found in the doctrine of the Manifesto and which critical communism has since developed by a broad and detailed analysis of the actual world, has certainly taken on by reason of the circumstances in which it was produced a warlike appearance and a very aggressive form. But it did not imply, any more than it implies now, either a chronological datum or a*

---

17 Labriola, *Essays*, 190.

prophetic picture of the social organization like those in the apocalypses and the ancient prophesies.[18]

Nevertheless, although this doctrine doesn't imply the year of the beginning of the new social structure, or its exact arrangement, it does imply (and this is what matters) the new form that inevitably follows the present one. "The foresight indicated by the Manifesto was not chronological, it was not a prophecy nor a promise, but a morphological prevision."[19]

Now with such a prediction, even if simply morphological, that is to say no more utopian but scientific prevision (as it's made by the very same society that, as Labriola says, "at a moment of its general process discovers the cause of its destined course"),[20] can it take place if not based on the intuition of the general and necessary development of history?

We like to follow up this question with the following passages of the first essay of Labriola:

> [T]he question was to recognize, or not to recognize, in the course of human events the necessity which stands over and above our sympathy and our subjective assent. Is or is not society in the countries most advanced in civilization organized in such a way that it will pass into communism by the laws inherent in its own future ...?
>
> Our aims are rational, not because they are founded on arguments drawn from the reasoning of reason, but because they are derived from the objective study of things, that is to say, from the explanation of their process, which is not, and which cannot be, a result of our will but which on the contrary triumphs over our will and subdues it. . . .

---

18 Ibid., 44.
19 Ibid., 45.
20 Ibid.

> [*The* Manifesto] *is a revolution—but not in the sense of an apocalypse or a promised millennium. It is the scientific and reflected revelation of the way which our civil society is traversing.* . . .
>
> *This historic conception, which gave a theoretic form to this necessity of the* new *social revolution more or less explicit in the instinctive consciousness of the proletariat and in its passionate and spontaneous movements, recognizing the intrinsic and imminent necessity of the revolution, changed the concept of it. That which the sects of conspirators had regarded as belonging to the domain of the will and capable of being constructed at pleasure, became a simple process which might be favored, sustained and assisted.* . . .
>
> *Ours is the* organic conception *of history. The* totality *of the* unity *of social life is the subject matter present to our minds.*[21]

But let us overlook the expressions and the explicit assertions; which would already be enough to precisely define Labriola's mindset and the range of the doctrine he presented. And let us get to the point of the matter.

Marx deserves credit for having understood—following Hegel—that human history is a process of becoming by antithesis, and for having seen—opposing Hegel—that it is not the Idea or any other abstract thing that develops dialectically, but society itself; that is, society in what is essential and original in itself, the economic fact, on which all social phenomena depend and derive. Two things must therefore be distinguished in Marx's historical doctrine: the first, borrowed from Hegel, which is the dialectical procedure; and the second, the content or subject of this procedure, which is opposed to that of Hegel. Therefore, there are two aspects from which the doctrine itself must be considered by those who wish to attempt a theoretical evaluation: the aspect of form and the aspect of content.

---

21 Ibid., 17, 18, 27, 29, 85–6.

And as far as the form is concerned, it should first be noted that historical materialism also intends to determine a process. To determine, let us say: although Labriola may prefer saying to see or to surprise, or another verb that better expresses that objectivity of the new intuition, which is so dear to him, as a singular quality and prerogative of the materialistic conception of history. To determine scientifically is not the same as reasoning in the abstract, running after the demands of logic, and then pretending at all costs to make history walk on the stilts of our reasoning. Oh! History goes on by itself, and even lets us enjoy ourselves on our own stilts.

Isn't historical materialism a theory of history as well, but also a conception, an interpretation of it? And aren't theory, conception, and interpretation all subjective operations, or rather, in this case, operations of the mind of Karl Marx and of the critical communists, or rather of a few or very few of them? et Labriola speak of the *self-criticism that is in things themselves*. It is a purely metaphorical phrase, like many others used by him; which, if it means that historical materialism itself, according to the theory it advocates, is the ideological product of the real conditions, i.e. the economic conditions of society, it cannot, to be logical, not also repeat itself of any philosophy of history, past or future, whether metaphysical or theological, which has a historical date, which is remembered, i.e. in the series of historical events; each of which, as it has its place, must also have its reason for being. It is certain that in things, in history, understood as something external and independent of us, there is neither meaning nor law; but it is always we who see a history with a meaning, with a law according to which we think it moves; it is always we, in short, who shape history and the law that governs it.

Of this subjectivity, before which our philosophers of the first half of the century veiled so much—to whom we owe so much, ungrateful as we are for lack of conscience! Of this subjectivity, which Kant discovered, after so much criticism that has been exercised on it, it should no longer be the case to worry, because it does not differ a single point (except in the scientific accuracy of the word) from that objectivity, which Labriola so often invokes, and which he is pleased to recognize in his doctrine. This observation is by now obvious and unnecessary for Professor Labriola; but it is opportune because of the great confusion of philosophical terms and of the history of philosophy which can be seen all around since the waters have been stirred up. Above all, it is opportune when we see that in a writing destined also in Italy for propaganda, Engels does not doubt to explain the idealism of Hegel, which would have been intrinsically outdated, writing thus:

> *Hegel was an idealist. To him the thoughts within his brain were not the more or less abstract pictures of actual things and processes, but, conversely, things and their evolution were only the realized pictures of the "Idea," existing somewhere from eternity before the world was. This way of thinking turned everything upside down, and completely reversed the actual connection of things in the world.*[22]

And so, Hegel repeats Plato, and consequently Kant says the same as Protagoras (and even worse, if we look at the most recent critique of the Democritus) and, to use an image of Hegel himself, we end up in the dark of night, when all the cows are black.

It has been said and it's usually repeated that whoever wants to understand Hegel's Logic should first read the *Phenomenology*, and remember that the key to this is in Kant's criticism. Now here Engels does not even suspect this historical need; and as we have seen, speaking of the Hegelian idea, he shows that he knows nothing of that subjectivity or humanity of science, which is equivalent, after Kant, to what is commonly called objectivity. We will return to this later.

---

22 Friedrich Engels, *Socialism: Utopian and Scientific*, trans. Edward Aveling (Chicago: Charles H. Kerr & Company: 1908), 86.

It is necessary, therefore, to leave the metaphors aside; and even when speaking of an objective, realistic, and materialistic theory of the historical process, to remember that what is meant is always a scientific elaboration (that is, such that it may succeed in being necessary for the minds of all and yet be valid as universal) *of our concepts* (production, form of production, exchange, society, etc.); ours no more and no less than that theological and metaphysical concept of Providence, from which the old philosophy of history made the course of human events governed by preordained ends.

Historical materialism, therefore, also determines a process of development, in which history must run. Now whoever says process is determinable *a priori*, says necessity of the process; and whoever says necessary process already establishes the basis of a prediction of the future, in a given form, at least, and to a given extent. And it should be noted that to arrive at this scientific predetermination of what bourgeois society is to become, is the main aim of the theorists of communism, because of the practical interests which animate their research. It is known that in the critique of the past they base the reason for the future, no longer, they say, vague or hoped for, but certainly expected, with the consciousness of its necessity. Necessity, Labriola warns, which does not come from a postulate of criticism, nor from destiny, nor from the command of law, but from the immanent process of history, *Objective necessity*, as he defines it elsewhere.

With all these characteristics, the materialistic conception of history cannot but be said to be a true philosophy of history. Except that Croce cautiously invites us to observe that:

The future stage of which some *speak with such certainty, as something that is not already conjectured but of which science* determines *the advent, has no character of necessity (subjective),*

that is, of certainty; just as the forecasts of history, not excluding the
same forecasts of socialism, can never have such a character.[23]

And elsewhere he warns against exaggerations, which in this case too may have been caused by that impulse, by that faith "which, as in the case of any practical work, accompanies the practical activities of socialism, and engenders beliefs and expectations which do not always agree with prudent critical and scientific thought."[24]

And here we really need to understand each other well. There is no science without prediction, that is, without laws that do not only include phenomena, and let's say past *events*, but also future phenomena, events yet to come. He who has a science in his hand, does not therefore become a prophet or an astrologer; and we all pity the poor Galileo who was forced to draw the horoscope, to serve the times and the wishes of the Great Duchess Cristina! But it is true that he sees a little further than others, whose visual virtue does not enhance any glass of science. That he sees, that is, that he must see into the future, is not in doubt: but what can he see? Here it is: all the single and concrete facts, and the temporal and spatial relations, and all the incidents of these facts do not fall within the domain of science, when they nevertheless escape from experience, because they are still to come. But beyond the facts, singularly considered with their particular relations, and beyond the accidents, there are the facts generally looked at in what is constant, necessary, and essential; which, determined especially for past facts, is also determinable *a priori* for future facts, and is like the form which these will take, when they are to happen. In this sense, science always gives rise to morphological predictions, and no more than these; so that, in order to define historical materialism as a philosophy of history, it may suffice that it arrives, as Prof. Labriola wants, at one of these predictions.

---

23 Croce, *Le teorie storiche*, 28.
24 Croce, *Historical Materialism*, 10–11.

Historical materialism, in order to have the right or the way to foresee the future form of society (whether near or remote, it doesn't matter; that historical periods determined by arithmetic, à la Ferrari and à la Bovio, are calculations made as a pastime!), should have grasped what is essential in the historical fact and seen the law of its real progress. What is essential in the historical fact is, for Hegel, the Idea, which develops dialectically; for Marx, the matter (the economic fact), which develops in the same way; and if Hegel with his Idea could make a philosophy of history, Marx can also make it; and he must be granted that his science, not the impulse of faith, makes him foresee what the present society is going to become, whenever it may be. The materialistic conception of history must know how to make this prediction, if it is true that it has discovered what is metaphorically called the substratum, and with less horror than old terms, one would say more properly the essence of history. It must know how to do it, because in the end it isn't a matter here of a prediction, but rather of a simple observation, and of a scientific observation, which must generate that certainty, that subjective necessity that Croce doesn't want to admit. The astronomer who foresees an eclipse of the moon or the sun, is not correct to say that he foresees it; because he does not see the future phenomenon, but the present phenomena which he knows from scientific experience will cause the future; and yet, speaking of these, he does nothing more than note the virtuality of the former. Now this virtuality of present society historical materialism says precisely that it has ascertained it, when it affirms that it is in front of what is *immanent* in the course of history. The immanent transcends the relations of time, and not even what is affirmed of it is therefore properly said to be foreseen; foresight presupposing that succession, which, at least as such, is the negation of the immanent. And here we have, or we should have, an immanent which is a perpetual becoming, the unity of succession and immanent, which is, however, always identical to itself in all moments of time, and can be seen in any of them, but speculatively and not experimentally, if historical materialism really looks at the substratum, at the essence of history. When it is said that ideologies do not explain history, but that it is they themselves that must be explained, and it is added that they are all explained by the economic conditions of society, one has already begun to philosophize; the experience is over. We must not, therefore, think of a prediction as an anticipation of what should be left to experience.

It is necessary, rather, to refer the circumstances to experience, which are like accidents, which always accompany phenomena, and which are not contemplated in the laws regulating them. But the circumstances, which often interfere with the regular course of the historical process, do not impair or spoil the character of the philosophical conception of historical materialism, which is praised for not putting aside and for-getting these circumstances: they, like the accidents of all phenomena, do not enter into the scientific elaboration of laws. Therefore, if Labriola is right in saying that "the genesis [of history, or of the struggle of economic classes that governs it—which is the same thing] foreshadowed,"[25] he will then be able to write about the circumstances that variously make up the historical process:

> *Thus the movement of history, taken in general, appears to us as it were oscillating;—or rather, to use a more appropriate image, it seems that it is unfolding on a line often interrupted, and at certain moments it seems to return upon itself, sometimes it stretches out, removing itself far from the point of departure:—in an actual zigzag.*[26]

But it must be pointed out, in order to be consequent, that this is such a *zigzag*, that its resultant turns out to be a straight line; that is to say (leaving the image) that historical circumstances do not operate on the economic substratum, and therefore cannot deviate its dialectical

---

25 Labriola, *Essays*, 192.
26 Ibid., 243.

movement, if they are superior constructions of the *economic man*; and if they are pertinent to the economic facts themselves, they themselves fall into the gear of those historical dialectics, which Marx has borrowed from Hegel. If this were not so, it would no longer be true that the economy is the essence of history, and that history is explained entirely by the variable conditions of history.

The circumstances, therefore, have nothing to do with the matter, which we wanted to discuss, of whether historical materialism was a new philosophy of history or not. If it were not such, we should add, how would it benefit socialism? and how would it have made it scientific from being utopian, as it was until Saint-Simon, as is being said? In fact, having removed that character of necessity from the historical process, which through the inevitable solution of the social antitheses must lead to the definitive communist order, what right do socialists have to appeal to this theory of history of theirs, in order to affirm that their ideal of society is no longer a hope to be cherished, a goal to which the conscious efforts of those who suffer should converge, but is already the necessary result of the same economic contradictions in which society finds itself at present in the most advanced nations? What would *Capital*, which is a critique of the past, have to do with critical communism, no longer utopianly vague in the manner of Fourier, and which would be a future state? Should it not have indicated two points in the history of the past which would determine a line which, prolonged in turn into the future, would lead to the democratic socialization of the means of production? Or else, how shall we say that historical materialism is the consciousness of contemporary socialism, and precisely the scientific consciousness?

"If historical materialism is stripped of every survival of finality and of the benignities of providence, it can afford no apology for either socialism or any other practical guidance for life."[27] These words of Benedetto Croce sound to our ear as a condemnation of the materialism of history as a socialist doctrine. They mean that this new doctrine has

---

27 Croce, *Historical Materialism*, 22.

not truly arrived, as they say, at the essence of the continuous historical course, at that dialectical immanent, which to be such, without finality and without providential plans, but by necessity of its nature, should ascend by the parable desired by the socialists, in the manner that from the embryo it develops little by little and climbs up and branches out and lives the plant. And beware of Croce who, if he applauds Marx's formula (*it is not the consciousness of men that determines their existence, but, on the contrary, their social existence determines their consciousness*), where, as we have seen, is the sum of all materialist theory, is he not right to write that:

> [I]n the assertion which can be made by its [historical socialism's] means, *its real and close connection with socialism is to be found. This assertion is as follows:—Society is now so constituted that socialism is the only possible solution which it contains within itself. An assertion and forecast of this kind moreover will need to be filled out before it can be a basis for practical action. It must be completed by motives of interest, or by ethical and sentimental motives, moral judgments and the enthusiasms of faith.*[28]

These other elements invoked by Croce are ideologies or effects of ideologies; and must they not, in both cases, germinate from the economic substratum? If they were independent, we would already have a confession of the insufficiency of the materialistic explanation of history; because we would have here nothing less than the greatest fact of history—the democratic socialization of all the means of production—produced by reasons that have nothing to do with the economic substratum, and belong rather to those ideal categories that have been mocked.

It should also be noted that when it is said that the scientific observation of socialism itself is limited to the observation that the only

---

28 Ibid.

possible solution that contains society as it is now shaped is socialism, we have not left the field of utopia, if we do not imply that the present conditions of society are themselves contradictory, so that a solution of the contradiction is, or at least appears *necessary*. Otherwise the proletarian who, in perfect conscience, makes the capitalist observe that socialism is the only possible solution, will be able to reply with a smile

Who told you that there must be a solution and that the face of the world must be changed, which, since its existence, has always counted servants and masters?—If we want to understand that there is only one possible solution or way out and that the solution or way out must necessarily be there, we fall at on our face into that necessity of historical conception from which Croce would like to subtract materialism and from which only socialism can draw that energy of scientific consciousness which it believes it can boast today.

But then, what about these other elements? They are there and must be there as a consequence of the very doctrine that historical materialism advocates. And how? This doctrine which discovers the source, hitherto unknown, of every religious form and of every morality, and which recognizes the characteristics of a bourgeois morality in that which is due to the *Critique of Practical Reason*, must it not also maintain that a period of social revolution due entirely to economic hardship and the greatest that history has matured—note that these revolutions are the pivots of history, according to historical materialism—also has a morality congruent with its real substratum? And if it fails in this point, which, as it is well said and clearly demonstrated, has matured this doctrine, to what is its value reduced?

This is indeed a serious objection that one thinks to make to those who hold historical materialism to a rigid or consequential philosophical or *a priori* conception. *Cave a consequentiariis!* The admonition in this case goes to the formers of the doctrine. It is observed that the conscious agitations of propaganda, with which they try to hasten the advent of the communist order, and the moral ideals to which the true socialist ideas must conform, intervene to take away from this rigor; ideals which are basically the cause and the motive of all propaganda.

Chiappelli sees, in this, an irreconcilable contradiction, pernicious to the same practical interests of socialism, which in fact strives to avoid it. In one of his essays, entitled *Idea morale nel socialismo* (The Moral Idea in Socialism), after having spoken about the absoluteness of the materialistic conception, he writes:

> *But the logic of things and of human life is stronger than the intentions of men. And not only, as is well known, did Malon oppose rigid Marxist materialism, but Liebknecht, one of the leaders of German socialism, warned in the Halle Congress: "Does not socialism contain the highest morality, anti-egoism, self-sacrifice, philanthropy?" This means that no resolution of the social problem could be initiated without referring to the moral nature of man, and without tacitly renouncing economic materialism.*[29]

And elsewhere he also observes:

> *A school or a party that wants to derive its rule of conduct from the doctrine of economic and social materialism, where it does not do with happy inconsistency the due reason to other elements (i.e., to moral impulses) runs the risk of converting the maxim from which socialism starts: "to each according to their own work," into the other: "to each according to their own needs," and ultimately substituting for this, at least implicitly, as Giddings noted, the other: "to each according to their own desires, which would mark the dissolution of every social order."*[30]

---

29 In Chiappelli, *Il Socialismo*, 227.
30 Ibid., 241.

Thus, Benedetto Croce reminds us that an eloquent commentary on the thought of Marx and Engels was their political action, with which they showed well that they were convinced of "the effectiveness of individual and collective efforts as cooperating and coordinating elements of objective forces,"[31] while theoretically, in the face of the utopians, they were forced to affirm that the so-called social question is not a moral question.

Vincenzo Gioberti, in his beautiful book *La Riforma cattolica* (The Catholic Reform)—which tells us what a fruitful and healthy religious movement the subalpine philosopher could have aroused, if his life had been enough, and if that industriousness which, until it died, seemed untiring, had not been broken—he excellently theorized that Catholicism must have an objective side that responds to every subjective quality, so that there are as many Catholicisms as there are human spirits, and foreseeing an obvious objection, he hastened to warn:

> *It will be said that the Pope, the bishops, etc., do not see Catholicism as I do. Those who make this objection do not understand me;* I reply that if they understood it in my way, I would not be right, but wrong.

Analogous to this objection is the difficulty of Chiappelli and Croce, to whom Marx and Engels could have replied: Precisely because of the rigorous character of the law that we have found in the overall progress of history, we have enthusiasm of faith, high moral ideals, and we feel strong impulses to work, to prepare or hasten the solution of the social antitheses; and our whole moral being, all the ideologies in which we participate, are a result of the present economic conditions of society. Just as, in order for Gioberti's doctrine on Catholicism to be true, he himself had to begin to understand it in his own personal and original way, and so had to do the pope himself, who represents the substance

---

31 Croce, *Le teorie storiche*, 29.

and the norm of Catholicism; thus, in order that historical materialism might not appear as a mere dream far from reality, it was good, it was obvious and natural, that its authors themselves should show that they had a morality and certain principles informing their practical life, such as they had to have or could have had in a historical period, which was already maturing an economic revolution, with its social and ideological forms. But just as it was not strictly necessary in Gioberti's theory that each person, in the proper sense of the word, should have his own particular Catholicism, and it was therefore not strictly contradictory to his theory that he did not fundamentally disagree with the Pope in his understanding of Catholicism, in the same way one cannot claim in an absolute way that Marx and Engels, in addition to being the theorists that they were, should also be those politicians and authors of propaganda that they also were. It is true that with that historical theory of theirs it was very difficult for them to remain skeptical or pessimistic, on the sidelines, and leave it to others; but what if they had had a different temperament? If Gioberti, in the event that he had published his work, and, forced by the hostile contradictions, which towards him alive would have been so much harsher than they were, had—an impossible hypothesis for that invincible soul of his!—had he disavowed his doctrine, humbly declaring that he understood Catholicism in the manner of the Pope and the bishops, the doctrine which he had genially begun would have been less true.

As far as historical materialism in particular is concerned, to Chiappelli and to those who would expect a materialistic practical morality of the theoretical conception that is said to be materialistic and to those who investigate whether, according to this doctrine, morality can become a vain *imaginatio*, it is enough to oppose a simple observation. Morality from the *Grundlegung zur Metaphysik der Sitten* onwards is, first of all, a fact. It does not have to be created by philosophy, but rather it has to be explained by philosophy; and only one can admit that theories radiate some reflection on actual morality. One can try to explain this *fact* by investigating its metaphysical, naturalistic, or materialistic foundation, but it is always what it is, with its own essence, and yet with certain general laws, constant and necessary among all men, which are such, among other things, because of their original ethical principle. Now what does it mean, towards historical materialism, as towards every philosophy of history, that morality is a *fact*? Fact means history; and history is what historical materialism must study and elucidate, not what it must produce; it is its content, its *presupposition*, not its *product*; and what is presupposed cannot be denied. Thus, in Greek history, materialism finds a very high and very elect ideology, Platonic idealism; in contemporary German history it finds another high and severe ideology, Hegel's absolute idealism. Well then, what is his position with respect to these two ideologies, the most remote from materialistic principles? He would renounce his most fundamental principle (*it is not the consciousness of men,* etc.) if he did not presume to discover a more or less close or distant origin and reason in the economic substratum of Greek and German history. And if in history there has been a place for the idealism of Plato and for that of Hegel, why should historical materialism not leave some for all idealisms and for all disinterested ethics that can ever form in the minds of men? To avoid this stumbling block, it is necessary to represent historical materialism not as having before it only the history that has happened—which is not the proper object of a philosophy of history—and almost as an instrument useful to give history a more rational course—which would return to the old utopias—but, as a science, which has for its object *the whole of history*, like every historical philosophy, and which, according to the image of Vico, among an immense ocean of doubts knows how to discern a single small land where one can stop his foot; from which there is a way to contemplate the course of history, seeing all that there is in it of immanent and necessary. Thus conceived, historical materialism must account for itself and for the whole of life; and as in life there is the beautiful and the good and the ugly and the bad, it must explain the beautiful and the ugly, and the good and the bad, that is, it must assign them a legitimate place. And since it is not a catechism, it cannot preach good or evil, that is, neither a utilitarian morality, as others believe, nor a disinterested morality, since it must keep to history, which is its object. It takes on the form and manner of a catechism when it warns of the importance of pedagogy in the formation of morals; and at the same time it leaves the proper sphere of a philosophy, losing sight of the first postulate of ethics: there is a morality among men.

But when the principle has been understood, that morality is a presupposition, and not a product of a historical doctrine, then it is to be believed that the objections inferred from the characters of socialist morality against the philosophical and absolute form of historical materialism can no longer be formulated.

Critique of the New Philosophy of History

Formally considered, the materialistic conception of history has such a philosophical character—we believe we have proved it—that it does not suffer any criticism of inconsistency. Finally, we would like to consider one of them, which is the most common one made about communism. And it too seems to us that it arises in the *form* of historical materialism, and is therefore completely worthless unless it is first shown that the very form of materialism is false, that is to say that it has a form which is contradictory to its content. Let us mention the criticism that runs with Wagner's concise phrase: socialism passes too quickly from the ideologies of the past to a hyper-ideology of the future.

Critical communists can respond to this criticism by saying that this ideology of the future, which seems to be a hyper-ideology, like so many other ideologies of the past that were really hyper-ideologies, does not depend on it, but they do not expect it to depend on the economic substratum, which will become capable of producing it. That socialism, if it sharpens the antagonism between the social classes, approaches precisely for this reason the end of the antagonism, fully ripening the internal contradiction which must be resolved; and as it is in their theory that the revolution is generated by the contradiction, once the contradictions are over, the leaven of every revolution will also have disappeared. The idea will have been fully realized; and there will be no more reason for the antitheses. It would indeed seem that the great philosophy of the absolute will throw its royal mantle over its prodigal son, historical materialism, as if to surround him with the sacred respect that his high speculation demands.

But up to now we have considered—and we really cared to concentrate on this—the form that historical materialism as a philosophy of history inherited from Hegel. It is time to add something about the new content that the author of the new doctrine wanted to give to the old form.

In this respect everyone repeats—I don't know with how much reason—that Hegelianism has been intrinsically surpassed; and everyone believes that this has happened because Hegel's principle has been replaced by the opposite principle, which would be in truth the one that was needed, since it is endowed with those characteristics that the dialectical process requires.

Except that it is clear that to make such a substitution it was necessary first to understand the value of the Hegelian Idea. And we have referred above to what Engels wrote about it in one of the most important documents for the formulation of this materialistic theory. In this theory the very contrast which is made between matter (reality, economic fact) and the Idea, already shows by itself that the Idea is conceived as transcending reality in the Platonic manner, in the act of developing according to logical laws which are equally transcendent, to which, as to the despotism of a sovereign exterior, the historical process should conform obediently.

Now the historians of philosophy know that nothing more false can be said in the interpretation of Hegelianism; for after the *Critique of Pure Reason* the Platonic hypostases and transcendences are banished from philosophy. The Idea, far from being opposed to reality, is, for Hegel, the essence of reality. Everything is to represent reality, as it is only possible after the teachings of Kant and after all the psychological studies of this century, which have done nothing but add the necessary complement that Kantianism expected from the side of psychology. And the matter of historical materialism, far from being external and opposed to Hegel's Idea, is included within it, indeed it is one and the same thing with it, since (this consequence Hegelianism drew from Kant's *a priori* synthesis!) the relative itself (which is the matter we are talking about) is not only not outside the absolute, but is identical with it, because of that unity of the many and the one, which Giordano Bruno had been able to point out from afar, but which had first to become, in order to be found, a problem of knowledge. The relative is indeed different from and opposed to the absolute; but it is a diversity, an opposition a thousand miles away from what these communist Hegelians suppose; who believe that the relative is, or rather has been made to be, by none other than Hegel himself, on one side, here, down below, one does not know where precisely, but it is said to be in reality, in history, and the absolute up there, in heaven perhaps, but one does not even know where precisely: the one in short facing the other, in two enemy camps, one against the other armed. They attribute this position to Hegel; because, in truth, by calling themselves materialists in the proper sense of the word, they believe they have thrown away the absolute, as an empty phantom, in order to keep to the fact, to the data of experience, that is to say, to the relative. But in any case, in contrast to the absolute of Hegel, such is also the position in which they represent their relative. And so, persuaded that they are in front of two different things, one of which does not exist, it was natural that they believed they could or should replace one of them with the other, the real with the imaginary. Nothing more reasonable.

But the trouble begins when, having made the substitution, the relative is forced to play the part of the absolute, as the historical materialists have the reasonableness to claim. The absolute is immanent; but the absolute is imaginary; the relative is real; therefore, the relative is immanent. The absolute develops dialectically; therefore, for the same reason as before, the relative develops dialectically. The process of the absolute was determined *a priori*, precisely because it was a dialectical process of the immanent; and yet it was also determinable *a priori*, and, as it were, the proper object of the philosophy of history, the relative. Not all of this, to tell the truth, they explicitly affirmed; but all of it is implicit, as we have seen, in their affirmations.

The relative, a matter proper to experience, determinable *a priori*? Here is the reason for all the difficulties of Croce: all of which can be resolved, since we believe we have resolved them, only by recognizing in historical materialism those characteristics of the philosophy of history, which then, in turn, necessarily lead to this absurdity: to make an *a priori* of what is empirical, to say that what must be referred to experience is determinable *a priori*, and therefore to predict, what Croce is right not to want to grant, a *fact*; since that form—which would give rise to the *morphological prediction*—what else would it be but a historical fact? The fact is not predicted, because it is not the object of speculation, but of experience; and therefore, does not belong to the philosophy of history, but to pure history (let us say history or historiography) which does not deal, as everyone knows, with anything but what has *already happened*.

And so, we must have a little patience, it seems, and wait until *the fact will have happened*, the form of society will have changed, and history will tell us for what reasons of antithesis to be resolved the revolution had to happen. For the moment we can only hope for it, and in good faith even wait for it; so that, if modern socialism is to be called "scientific," no longer utopian, it must be understood only in the sense that it, unlike the utopias that have already passed away, no longer addresses itself to metaphysical ideals of justice, or to forms of society equally conceived according to philosophical systems, but to the economic critique of social conditions; not in the sense in which it is most often accepted, that is, socialism, which already has the scientific (philosophical) consciousness of its necessity.

Therefore, in the end, historical materialism, if it wants to be more than a simple methodological view, useful to the historiographer, considered from the philosophical aspect it succeeds in being one of the most wretched deviations of Hegelian thought, in that it leads back to a metaphysics (necessary and absolute science) of reality, understood as an object in the pre-Kantian manner; and, what is more, it leads to the conception of a dialectic, determinable *a priori*, of the relative. But as a simple methodological view, does it really benefit the consciousness of critical communism?

— The Philosophy of Praxis —

I.

Philosophical Studies of Karl Marx

In the preface to his *A Contribution to the Critique of Political Economy* (1859) Marx recalled that in 1845 in Brussels, together with Engels, he had waited to put into practice a certain plan to define the position of their ideas—especially concerning, as Engels later warned, the materialistic conception of history—against the ideological theories of German philosophy, and to come to terms, so to speak, with previous philosophical knowledge "in the form of a criticism of post-Hegelian philosophy."[32] The result would be a manuscript for two large volumes in octavo, which, sent to a printer in Westphalia, remained in print, until the events that occurred prevented its publication. Marx concluded: "We abandoned the manuscript to the gnawing criticism of the rats; all the more willingly, since we had already achieved our purpose—which was to understand ourselves."[33]

Friedrich Engels, in connection with a long review he had written two years earlier of a memoir on Feuerbach, said in 1888 that he had taken up and looked over that old scrap of 1845–46; and he declared:

The part of it dealing with Feuerbach is not complete. The portion completed consists in an exposition of the materialistic view of

---

32 Marx, *Contribution to the Critique*, 13.
33 Ibid., 14.

> *history and only proves how incomplete at that time was our*
> *knowledge of economic history.*[34]

This information on the studies that were being carried out by the two socialist writers around 1845 is precious; and it is worthwhile, in our opinion, to resolve the question, discussed in the most recent literature on historical materialism, even in Italy: that is, whether in the mind of Marx and his Metrodorus this tormented materialistic conception of history arose with the characteristics of a philosophical theory, intrinsically coordinated with a new special system of true philosophy.

In that manuscript, which it would be useful to bring to light, because it would serve, more and better than any other of his works, to reconstruct historically the birth and development of Marx's thought, we know in the meantime, from the testimony of one of the authors themselves, that, for better or worse, the new conception of history was set forth, which was then to be perfected and formulated in the *Communist Manifesto*, and more consciously advocated in *A Contribution to the Critique of Political Economy*; and this conception was exposed in order to orient itself among the contemporary philosophical trends, and then develop a core of guiding principles that were the backbone of a new system. Marx says that in that work he clarified his own philosophical thought; and Engels adds that the new historical intuition already appeared. Whoever puts together the two testimonies, it seems to us that there can be no doubt of the scope with which it was outlined, already in 1845, historical materialism in the mind of Marx.

Now, while agreeing with Croce, that for the writings of Marx, more than for the writings of any other thinker:

> *[T]he interpreter must proceed with caution: he must do his work*
> *bit by bit, book by book, statement by statement, connecting indeed*

---

34 Engels, *Feuerbach*, 35.

*these various indications one with another, but taking account of
differences of time, of actual circumstances, of fleeting impressions,
of mental and literary habits; and he must submit to acknowledge
ambiguities and incompleteness where either exists, resisting the
temptation to confirm and complete by his own judgment.*[35]

While willingly accepting these prudent warnings, we believe that on the
basis of the news reported there is no doubt that a point has been
established, which must be the starting point of our investigation. In
which it is not a question, for the moment and in this case, of researching
what is critically acceptable at the bottom of historical materialism—a
very important research, but essentially critical, and yet completely
unrelated to the history of Marx's thought, which in any case must follow,
not precede it—but rather of studying how this theory, which he used as
the basis of a very serious social doctrine, was actually conceived by Marx.
And if Marx as well as Engels, referring to such a voluminous work, and
written when this theory was emerging in their minds and being formed,
explicitly declare that it took the form of a philosophical system, so as to
oppose contemporary systems, there is no prudence of interpretation
that can revoke in doubt the philosophical scope that was really
attributed to historical materialism, from the beginning, by the authors
themselves. This is not the case of an unconscious thought, which one
must be careful to trust; it is a matter of a deep mental work that takes
shape in a vast writing.

I therefore fully agree with Labriola, when he approves of Sorel's
intention to put back into the field the problem of philosophy in general,
giving himself the thought that:

*[H]istorical materialism may appear to be out of place until it has
other philosophies against it, with which it does not harmonize, and
until a way is found to develop the philosophy which is proper to it,*

---

35 Croce, *Historical Materialism*, 80.

as that which is inherent and immanent to its assumptions and premises.[36]

He believes, therefore, that he is carrying out the concept of this philosophy, proper to historical materialism in the mind of Marx himself. What in fact he tried to do in his letters to Sorel, attempting at the same time to determine the orientation of Marxism among today's philosophical directions.

But since there are many, around Labriola, *liacos intra muros*, who believe that he has, against the intentions of Marx, widened the scope of the materialistic doctrine of history without good foundation, it will be useful to put forward the documents of the genuine thought of Marx himself.

---

36 Labriola, *Discorrendo di socialismo e di filosofia* (Rome: Loescher, 1897), letter V, 58.

II.

Marx's Critique of Feuerbach

As an appendix to his writings on Feuerbach, Friedrich Engels published eleven of Marx's theses or fragments on that philosopher, written in Brussels in January 1845, and rediscovered by Engels in one his friend's old notebooks.

"These are," he writes, "notes hurriedly scribbled in for later elaboration, not in the least degree prepared for the press, but invaluable, as the first written form, in which is planted the genial germ of the new philosophy [*der neuen Weltanschauung*]."[37] These notes of Marx refer to Feuerbach's Essence of Christianity, and indicate the evolution of the disciple with respect to the master, and thus the historical relations of Marxism with the degenerate Hegelianism of the left, represented especially by Feuerbach. It is therefore worth briefly recalling the characteristics of this philosophy, according to the work now cited.

For Hegel, philosophy and faith can and must get along: the same content is in both, in a different form. It has been observed that in this way he contradicted one of the fundamental principles of his logic: there must always be perfect parallelism between form and content. This is an unfair criticism, because Hegel did not deny the transformation of content into different forms; nor, therefore, that content and form in philosophy, and content and form in religion, proceeded from one another and with perfect correlation. He did not deny, I say, the diversity

---

37 Engels, *Feuerbach*, 36.

of the concrete contents, as they are implemented in the two different forms; but he affirmed the identity of the content abstractly considered, insofar as it is considered transcendentally separate and of the philosophical form and the religious form. On the other hand, according to Hegel: "The form of feeling [*proper to religion*] is the lowest in which spiritual truth can be expressed. The world of spiritual existences, God himself, exists in proper truth, only in thought and as thought."[38]

Feuerbach, however, in *Essence of Christianity* (1841) opposed this sentence, stating that between philosophy and religion there is a diametrical opposition, as between the healthy and the infirm; one being produced by thought, the other by imagination and feeling. Faith and science cannot be composed, therefore, to friendly peace. Hegel had said that man recognizes himself in his God; it is to say, however, that God knows himself in man. That is to say: in religion man does not want to know himself, nor even to know himself incompletely (to represent himself); he wants rather to satisfy himself in his physical needs. In what, in fact, is man's individual essence? In a continuous satisfaction of his own organic needs. And this he wants to find in God. The egoistic feeling, badly satisfied with the faintness of real life, pushes man to sublimate himself in an in finite power, which is divine power, omnipotence to satisfy all his needs. Man, therefore, through religion does not recognize himself, as a spirit, as an absolute, as universal, in God, but this absolute, spirit, universal, must, however, be recognized in particular individual, which as a physical organism lives through the incessant event of the emergence and satisfaction of needs. Not therefore the truth of the individual is in the universal, but the truth of this is in the individual. Matter does not merge into spirit, but matter in spirit. Hegelian idealism turned upside down.

And since the root of religion is to be found in man as a physical individual, theology is transformed into anthropology; and this is

---

38 Georg Wilhelm Friedrich Hegel, *The Logic of Hegel*, trans. William Wallace (Oxford University Press, 1892), 33–34.

essentially materialistic. The needs which stimulate the fantasies of the deification of human powers elevated to infinity, are in fact physical needs; and the essence of man therefore comes to be determined as purely physical and organic.

The critique of religion, therefore, was based on materialism. In fact, in *Principles of the Philosophy of the Future* (1843) Feuerbach teaches that true philosophy can only be empirical, having as its object the sensible reality. The deepest and most important truths cannot be learned except by the way of the senses. And philosophy must not consider man as thought or reason, but for what he *really* is, a concrete sensible being, a living body. The Ego is precisely the body. So that philosophy itself, insofar as it has man as its object, succeeds in a physiological anthropology.

Like religion, all the facts that are considered the highest and noblest of human life and society are products of man as an organic body, which lives by the continuous satisfaction of its needs.

The consequence of this philosophy is obvious: all history can have no other well-founded explanation than a materialistic one. Look for and study the needs of the human body in its actual existence and you will have the reason for all human facts, small or great, individual or social. It is understood that the explanation of individual facts is to be sought in the immediate physical needs of the individual as such; whereas the explanation of social facts must come from the analysis of the needs of the individual as a member of society, or rather of a given society. If Feuerbach formulated his materialism with a typical expression by saying that *man is no more and no less than what he eats (der Mensch sei nur das, was er esse)*, and the explanation, therefore, of his work, as a pure and simple individual, can only be given by the needs of his stomach, the explanation of his historical facts can only arise from economic needs.

This is how historical materialism descended with plain and evident logic from the materialism of Feuerbach. No other philosophy than materialism can therefore be considered immanent in the materialistic conception of history. But let us see what observations Marx made about this philosophy as he prepared in 1845 to write about his own philosophical orientation. And therefore, we give here, translated as best we can, the fragments printed by Engels:

I.

*The chief lack of all materialistic philosophy up to the present, including that of Feuerbach, is that the thing, the reality, sensation is only conceived of under the form of the object which is presented to the eye, but not as human sense-activity, "praxis," not subjectively. It therefore came about that the active side in opposition to materialism was developed from idealism, but only abstractly; this was natural, since idealism does not recognize real tangible facts as such. Feuerbach is willing, it is true, to distinguish objects of sensation from objects existing in thought, but he conceives of human activity itself not as objective activity. He, therefore, in the "Wesen des Christenthums," [*Essence of Christianity*] regards only theoretical activity as generally human, while the "praxis" is conceived and fixed only in its disgusting form.*

II.

The question if objective truth is possible to human thought is not a theoretical but a practical question. In practice man must prove the truth, that is the reality and force in his actual thoughts. The dispute as to the reality or non-reality of thought which separates itself, "the praxis," is a purely scholastic question.

III.

The materialistic doctrine that men are the products of conditions and education, different men therefore the products of other conditions and changed education, forgets that circumstances may be altered by men and that the educator has himself to be educated.

It necessarily happens therefore that society is divided into two parts, of which one is elevated above society (Robert Owen for example).

The occurrence simultaneously of a change in conditions and human activity can only be comprehended and rationally understood as a revolutionary fact.

IV.

Feuerbach proceeds from a religious self-alienation, the duplication of the world into a religious, imaginary, and a real world. His work consists in the discovery of the material foundations of the religious world. He overlooked the fact that after carrying this to completion the important matter still remains unaccomplished. The fact that the material foundation annuls itself and establishes for itself a realm in the clouds can only be explained from the heterogeneity and self-contradiction of the material foundation. This itself must first become understood in its contradictions and so become thoroughly revolutionized by the elimination of the contradiction. After the earthly family has been discovered as the secret of the Holy Family, one must have theoretically criticized and theoretically revolutionized it beforehand.

V.

Feuerbach, not satisfied with abstract thought, invokes impressions produced by the senses, but does not comprehend sensation as practical sensory activities.

VI.

Feuerbach dissolves religion in humanity. But humanity is not an abstraction dwelling in each individual. In its reality it is the ensemble of the conditions of society.

Feuerbach, who does not enquire into this fact, is therefore compelled:

1. *To abstract religious sentiment from the course of history, to place it by itself, and to pre-suppose an abstract, isolated, human individual.*
2. *Humanity is therefore only comprehended by him as a species, as a hidden sort of merely natural identity of qualities in which many individuals are embraced.*

VII.

Therefore Feuerbach does not see that religious feeling is itself a product of society, and that the abstract individual which he analyses belongs in reality to a certain form of society.

VIII.

The life of society is essentially practical. All the mysteries which seduce speculative thought into mysticism find their solution in human practice and in concepts of this practice.

IX.

The highest point to which materialism attains, that is the materialism which comprehends sensation, not as a practical fact, is the point of view of the single individual in bourgeois society.

X.

The standpoint of the old materialism is "bourgeois" society; the standpoint of the new, human society, or associated humanity.

XI.

Philosophers have only interpreted the world differently, but the point is to change it.[39]

---

39 Engels, *Feuerbach*, 129–133.

In these faithfully translated thoughts, it does not seem difficult for us to see the design of a whole new speculative system, with its history entangled in an earlier philosophy, and with sure hints of a practical program being logically consequent: the whole skeleton in short of that philosophy, which is believed to be inherent in the conception of historical materialism, placed at the foundation of the communist doctrine. And here we will try with the help of these thoughts to provide a sketch of this new philosophy.

III.

Sketch of the Philosophy of Praxis

The keystone of this philosophical construction lies in the concept of "praxis." This concept, as Marx himself well notes, is new with respect to materialism, but in idealism it is as old as idealism itself; indeed, it was born in childbirth with it, right from the subjectivism of Socrates. Socrates could not conceive of a truth already beautiful and formed, that could be transmitted by tradition or teaching; and he thought instead that every truth is the final result of personal inquisitive work, in which the master can only act as a companion and collaborator to the disciple desirous of the truth. Hence the famous comparison of his art with the maieutic art of his mother Fenarete. He did not produce knowledge in the minds of the disciples; but they were only helped by him to form, to make this knowledge. Helped in praxis, Marx would say. Knowledge, therefore, was already for Socrates a productive activity, and was a subjective construction, a continuous and progressive praxis.

Nor did Plato let this very important doctrine slip away; on the contrary, he better defined it and developed it in his dialectic of ideas, all of which are endowed with creative energy. And up to Hegel there was no idealist who did not understand, more or less well, knowledge as a work of the human spirit, with the exception of the rare supporters of intellectual intuition.

Our Vico, usually boasted only as the founder of the philosophy of history, saw very deep into this matter. And in this concept of cognition as praxis lies the whole reason for his inexorable criticism of Descartes. To whom the Neapolitan philosopher could not forgive the fact that he had set as the starting point and foundation of science the immediate consciousness of thought (*cogito ergo sum*); where, according to him, when we do science, we must justify the fact of consciousness, re-constructing its birth and development: that is, not starting from the pure fact, but, as we now say, starting from the explanation of the fact itself, remaking it ourselves. *Verum et factum convertuntur*; truth, therefore, is discovered by doing it. And since it is the result, and not the given, of scientific research, this cannot proceed by analysis, as Descartes claims, which would presuppose before itself the concept of the truth to be analyzed, but by synthesis, which is the productive activity of the mind. Hence the inestimable value of the divinations of the genius, of the happy intuitions, which create, almost, rather than make, the knowledge, so difficult to acquire. According to Vico, doing is the unchangeable condition of knowing. Hence the certainty of mathematics—and in this he agreed with Descartes—in which the objects of our knowledge are not given, but constructed.

These principles, already enunciated in the work *On the Most Ancient Wisdom of the Italians* (1710), he then had to admirably apply in the New Science, in constructing his historical philosophy. And in truth, if one can know what is one's own work, the natural world is to be referred, Vico thought, to the cognition of God, who is its only factor; but the historical world, the product of human activity, is the object of which men who have made it can achieve science. But for Vico this human activity was the activity of the mind of man; hence his concept that all history could be explained by the consideration and study of the modifications of the mind. The principle of operation changes in Marx, and instead of changes in the mind, the needs of the individual as a social being are the root of history. But the concept that is invoked of praxis remains the same.

Nor does it suffer criticism or correction. Labriola says very well that "thinking is producing. Learning is producing by reproducing. We only know what we ourselves are capable of producing, by thinking, working, trying and trying again; and always by virtue of the forces that are our own, in the social field and from the visual angle in which we find ourselves."[40] What is the experiment, if not a remaking of what nature does, remaking it in conditions that facilitate and ensure the observation? Of course, this doing or remaking is not always a material and effective doing; on the contrary, most of the time it is purely a doing or remaking with thought. But does the same material and effective doing or remaking benefit the understanding of the fact because of the immediate mechanism, or not rather because of the gradual thinking of the individual parts of the mechanism? The answer is easy for those who consider that the mind has neither eyes nor hands nor instruments, except by metaphor; and the mechanics of external making cannot be accompanied except by successive representations. This original activity, which must be developed for the attainment of science, is most evident, e.g., in arithmetic calculation. You have the factors; you are looking for the product. This product is not a product which you have glimpsed by intuition; it is the result of an operation which you must perform. And what is said of this arithmetical product must be said of every product of knowledge, of all knowledge: it is not given, but must be arrived at by the active act of the mind. Given knowledge is not true knowledge if it is not understood, that is, if it is not true knowledge if it is not understood, that is, if it is not reconstructed; and therefore, it is no longer given, but produced or reproduced.

And is science, in general, acquired all of a sudden, as if by a very sharp glance cast around a wide horizon? The remaking will be easier than the doing; and reading a scientific book is easier than writing it. But even in reading our spirit, if it wants to profit, cannot remain inert and passive; on the contrary it must accompany the intelligence of the author,

---

40 Labriola, *Discorrendo di socialismo*, 43.

in every moment of his progress, and therefore it too must develop an energy, and *do* it too. In the language one can already see traces of this very important concept of knowing or understanding that is a doing. The Latin word *facilis* (which remains in all Romance languages) derives from the verb *facere*; and etymologically therefore it would only mean "that can be done." Where, in Latin and in all Romance languages, it also means that can be known or understood. Thus an operation is easy to do; and a truth is easy to know, or a theorem to understand.

This concept that knowledge goes hand in hand with activity, with praxis, is the soul of Froebel's pedagogical method. "The starting point for him was doing, which is behind knowing; and knowledge is none other than the genetic development of doing itself."[41] But Froebel did not derive this principle from a materialistic philosophy either; on the contrary, it has been well observed that "the *thun* (doing), and the *genetisch-entwickelnd* method (of genetic development) so inculcated by Froebel effortlessly call to mind that doctrine [of Fichte] which from the primitive doing of the Ego attempted to develop all our science."[42]

This principle wants Marx to transport abstract idealism into concrete materialism. He judges it to have been a very serious defect, indeed the main one, to have neglected it.

This concept demonstrates the philosophical acumen of the writer. In truth, what was, after all, the reproach he made against materialism in the theory of knowledge? This: to believe that the object, the sensitive intuition, the external reality is a *datum*, instead of a *product*; so that the subject, entering into relationship with it, should limit himself to a pure vision, or rather to a simple mirroring, remaining in a state of simple passivity. Marx, in short, reproached the materialists, and among them Feuerbach, for conceiving the subject and the object of knowledge in an abstract and false position. In such a position one would have the object

---

41 Francesco Fiorentino, "Friedrich Fröbel," in *Giornale napoletano di filosofia e lettere, scienze morali e politiche* (Napoli: Riccardo Marghieri, 1878), 220.
42 Ibid.

opposed to the subject and without any intrinsic relation to it, which is accidentally encountered, seen, known. But what is this subject without its object? And this object without the respective subject, of which is it the object? Subject and object are also two correlative terms, one of which necessarily draws behind the other. They are therefore not mutually independent, but rather inseparably linked to each other, so that their actual reality results from their relationship to the organism in which and through which they find their necessary fulfillment, and outside of which they are nothing but abstractions. The life of the subject is in its intrinsic relation to the object; and vice versa. Sever this relation; and you will no longer have life, but death. No longer two real terms of the fact of knowing, but two abstract terms.

They must therefore be conceived in their mutual relation. The nature of this relationship is made clear by what has been said about the activity of knowing. When one knows, one makes the object, and when one makes or constructs an object, one knows it; therefore the object is a product of the subject; and, since there is no subject without an object, it must be added that the subject, as he comes to make or construct the object, comes to make or construct himself; the moments of the progressive formation of the subject correspond to the different moments of the progressive formation of the object.

He who has known little is said to have developed his ideas, his thought; and as he increases his knowledge (object), he grows in the power of comprehension and understanding (subject). Knowledge, in short, is a continuous development; and, since it is essentially but a relation of two correlative terms, it amounts to a progressive parallel development of these two terms. The root meanwhile, the permanent cause of this development is in the activity, the doing of the subject, which forms itself, forming the object; *crescit et concrescit*; ἐπίδοσις ἐφ'αὑτῷ (Aristotle).[43]

---

43 Latin is "increases and grows"; Greek is "growth within itself."

Now, when materialism says: the spirit is a *tabula rasa*, on which the images of the external world are gradually written through the action of the senses; one thinks on the one hand of this *tabula rasa*, ready to receive the images of the external world; on the other hand, of the objects of this world, beautiful and formed, accomplished in themselves, which, if it falls to them to send images to that *tabula rasa*, send them; and if not, they remain what they are, without any loss of themselves, as they would have gained nothing from sending the images.

Here is the abstract position of materialism; it does not stand up to the most elementary criticism. Who describes the images on the *tabula rasa*? Is it the subject that forms them, or the object? And if the subject and the object exist, without these images, a product of the relation into which they may enter, if they exist therefore independent of each other, who is subject, as pure subject, and who is object as pure object? Questions which materialism can in no way answer without contradicting its presuppositions; for, it is known, an abstract cannot receive any determination, without conceiving itself in the conditions in which and for which it is concrete; that is, without denying itself as abstract.

Rather, we must recognize the legitimate motive that suggests such a position: the so-called objectivity of knowledge, whereby the object must be an object, pure object, without mixture of subjectivity. Because if knowledge acquires value from the object of which it gives us possession, this value no longer has it when the object is altered by the influence or contact of the subject, which must be the knowing principle opposed to the known. Hence the theory of intuitions, simple visions that make the sensible image of external objects pass into our spirit without the slightest modification. Therefore, pure object and intuition are the characteristics of objectivism—idealistic or materialistic—to which Marx wants to oppose subjectivism. Reality has hitherto been conceived, he says, as *object, intuition*, not as human activity, as *praxis*, not *subjectively*. Reality then, according to him, is a subjective production of man; a production, however, of sensory activity (*sinnliche Tätigkeit*); not of thought, as Hegel and the other idealists believed.

From Feuerbach, therefore, go back to Hegel, who understood an indisputable truth: that knowledge is a continuous production, an incessant doing, an original praxis. But this his principle from the abstract idealistic conception of the spirit transfer to the real and concrete human sensory activity. Idealism did not deny sense; but it did not recognize it as such, but rather as a moment of thought, which is not active, productive as sense, but only as thought.

Now Feuerbach, in his *Essence of Christianity*, what did he do? He distinguished the Judaic forms of Christianity from its theoretical content; those products of praxis, this pure product of human thought: an absolute duality between fact and theory, between praxis and knowledge, which are instead one and the same thing. Feuerbach, in short, was not consequent to himself: he explained in a materialistic way the practical part of the history of Christianity; but he stopped before the ideologies, that is to say the speculative part, the last stronghold opposed to him by idealism and not conquered by him. And in this regard, before the same problem, Labriola observes:

> *It is the difficult understanding of how ideologies arise from the material ground of life, which gives strength to the argument of those who deny the possibility of a full genetic* (materialistic) *explanation of Christianity. In general, it is true that phenomenology or religious psychology, as it may be called, presents great difficulties and contains some very obscure points. . . . But is this psychological difficulty a privilege of Christian beliefs? Is it not proper to the generation of all mythical and religious beliefs and ideas. . . . The fact is that these psychic productions of the men of past centuries present special difficulties to our understanding. We cannot easily reproduce in ourselves the conditions that are necessary to approach the inner state of mind, which was respective*

to those products. . . . Except that Christianity (and here I mean belief, doctrine, myth, symbol, legend, and not mere association in its oikonomika), *is relatively easier for us, since it is closer to us. We live in the midst of it, and we are constantly considering its consequences and derivations in the literature and various philosophies familiar to us. We can, however, observe how the multitudes combine, wholesale, both the atavistic and the recent superstitions with a half-hearted or barely approximate acceptance of the most general principle, which unifies all confessions—the fall and redemption. We see the Christian association at work, as much in what it does as in the struggles it sustains, and we are able to refer to the past by analogical combinations, which we seldom succeed in employing in the interpretation of beliefs remote from us. We still witness the creation of new dogmas, of new saints, of new miracles, of new pilgrimages; and, thinking back on the past, we can for the most part say:* tout comme chez nous![44]

Well, do we not see that all these questions originate from interests, from material needs? These practical interests, these material needs have as their object the sensible reality, which they tend to procure, to do. Now their object is not really distinct and separate from the object of thought, as Feuerbach believes and wants it to be (*sinnliche, von den Gedankenobjekten wirklich unterschiedene Objekte*); for, if this were so, materialism would not be able to explain the whole work of man. This may seem to be of a double nature, practical and theoretical, to those who have not understood the concept of knowing as doing. But when doing is unified with knowing, the objects proper to knowing are also objects of doing, and vice versa; so that there is finally a single class of objects, relative to praxis (which is doing and knowing together) and produced by it. And if materialism suffices for the explanation of the objects *made*,

---

44 Labriola, *Discorrendo di socialismo*, 123–5.

it must also suffice for the explanation of the objects *known*, which are, after all, of the same nature as the former. Feuerbach's doctrinal constructions are explained by the abstract activity of the spirit, the true human activity, according to him; and thus he falls squarely within that idealism which he had resolutely denied.

Also according to Feuerbach, therefore, human activity is not properly objective (*gegenständliche Tätigkeit*), it does not produce objects opposed to man; but only objects, so to speak, subjective: knowledge, not facts. And with respect to knowing the true objects, that is, the sensible reality remains absolutely foreign to thought, independent of it. Feuerbach's capital error is that he was not consistent with himself; he introduced a duality into the very bosom of materialism, which is an essentially monistic philosophy, because he was unable to recognize the productive character of sensory activity, the shaper of all reality.

It is necessary, in short, to fulfill the materialistic intuition with the very fertile concept of the practical-critical energy; of the energy that is expressed by producing and knowing simultaneously what it produces: the new concept of the "revolutionaries."

IV.

Realism of the Philosophy of Praxis

Thus the abstract is replaced by the concrete. The object, produced by human activity, fantasized independent of man, is replaced by the object intrinsically linked to human activity, which is developed in a process parallel to the process of its development. True realism begins.

And in this realism the scholastic questions, which wandered about the relation of abstracts as such, are forever denied. In what way, it was asked before, does the object reach the subject, or vice versa? In what way can objectivity, the reality of knowing, be explained? And so asking, of course, one wanted to derive a (real) relation from the abstract nature of the two terms. Now, it is clear that when these two terms are conceived in their proper, concrete condition of the mutual relationship of cause and effect, of activity and product, from which we have seen that they are bound to each other, those questions no longer have any reason to be. Thought is real because and insofar as it poses the object. Either thought is, and thinks; or it does not think, and is not thought. If it thinks, it does. Therefore reality, the objectivity of thought, is a consequence of its very nature. This is one of the first consequences of Marxist realism.

But pay attention to the meaning of thought, as it is determined in this philosophy. This philosophy wants to be materialistic, and therefore cannot admit thought as such: on the contrary, thought is considered a derived and accidental form of the sensory activity. This is the original activity; and in it therefore is the root and substance of thought.

Therefore, when we speak of thought, no matter what we say, we always mean to speak of the ordinary conscious form of an original unconscious activity, which is the psychic. The organism of thought is none other than the organism of this activity, to which it is always necessary to refer in order to realize what is considered to be the product of thought, and therefore of all history.

But in this realistic materialism another of the main doctrines of abstract materialism is also corrected. All the materialists of the last century, and not a few of those who came after these speculations of Marx, hold that man is a product of environment and education. Helvétius and Rousseau, for example, denied any original difference between human traits, which are then differentiated in society. Montesquieu drew attention to the great influence of climates on the life of peoples; Cabanis, together with the ideologists, endeavored to demonstrate in general the relationship of the physical to the moral, the physical considering the effect of the moral. What are the consequences of these materialistic theories with respect to communistic theories? Here is Robert Owen, the great utopian, who accepts the ideas of these, and moved by a deep philanthropic feeling, criticizes the society that pretends to virtuous men by putting them in circumstances, which necessarily spoil the good native dispositions, and drag them to vice and crime; and advocates by example and theory the moral obligation to provide everyone with the appropriate conditions for a healthy formation of character. But whose obligation is this? Society itself, which should be modified according to the criteria of these doctrines. Thus society would come to be divided into two distinct parts, one above the other and the cause of the latter's conduct. What in fact is an organic whole would become a disjointed whole of parts. The abstract would again take the place of the concrete. The truth is that these circumstances, whose influence determines the conduct and character of men, are themselves determined by men; and education itself supposes the educators, who must have been educated. The cause presupposes the effect, and is itself the effect.

What does this riddle mean? Society, which is an organic whole, is both cause and effect of its conditions; and we must seek in the very bosom of society the reason for all its changes.

There is the society that educates, and there is the society that is educated: the same society, which has already been educated, returns to educate. All education is therefore a practice of society, a continuous activity of man, who *crescit*, as we said, and *concrescit*; he educates, educating himself, and gradually increasing his own educating capacity. Thus, if circumstances form man, and are themselves formed by man, it is always man who operates by determining circumstances, which then react on him.

But, it is said however, the man who operates, is the social man, the society; the man on whom the circumstances react, is the individual. Except that, is there really this individual abstracted from society, or is it a creation of fantasy? Where is this man determined by circumstances, (social), if not in society? In truth the man we know is the social man. Nor is there any man who is in society and does not act upon it; just as there is no man upon whom the society in which he lives does not react.

The theory of the environment is therefore undermined by the new realism, which does not disavow materialism, but rather wants to confirm it and make it more and more logical. It wants to correct the abstract position in which materialists and utopians had placed man in front of the environment. Having conceived man in his real relationship with society, it is easy to rise from the dualism of environment and individual to the rigorous monism of materialism. The activity of praxis, the only original activity is—given the nature of the relation between subject and object—the productive energy of the object; and it has perfectly parallel moments of development. Now if this praxis is knowing and doing, the objects of it are theoretical and practical, they are knowledge and facts; hence also circumstances, education, environment.

But as the object grows, progresses, and changes, the subject also grows, progresses, and changes in parallel, due to the fact that the object itself grows, progresses, and changes. Therefore the effect reacts on the cause, and their relationship is reversed, the effect becoming the cause of the cause, which becomes an effect while remaining a cause; and there is, in short, a synthesis of cause and effect. Praxis, which had the subject as its principle and the object as its term, is reversed, returning from the object (principle) to the subject (term). And yet Marx noted that the coincidence of changing circumstances and human activity can be conceived and rationally explained only as praxis that reverses itself (*nur als umwälzende Praxis*).

In short, it is the usual rhythm already described (and not only described!) by idealism—the only direction that had developed until Marx, the principle of praxis—in the field, however, of abstract thought. Fichte said *thesis, antithesis, synthesis; being, not being, becoming,* Hegel said. And keeping an eye precisely on real life, Froebel, following in the footsteps of Fichte, had also established his triad, always with the same dialectical meaning: *Satz, Gegensatz, Vermittlung; living, doing, knowing.*

The subject, Marx's practical activity, is the thesis; circumstances and education are the antithesis; the subject modified by circumstances and education, the synthesis. And since the subject is the original activity which posits the object, it is also the being, which denies itself by positing the object, since this position is a single determination of its activity; and, as Spinoza said, *omnis determinatici est negatio.* The object therefore (circumstances, education) is equivalent to the Hegelian non-being; the contradiction of which, intrinsic to being, produces the becoming of being itself, that is, of the subject which is, as has been said, modified by the object (circumstances, education).

So that also in this way the correction of materialism consists in an application to matter of what Hegel had exactly discovered with respect to the spirit. For Marx does no more than substitute matter for thought; but matter that is endowed with the same activity which was once considered the privilege of thought; and this activity he endeavors to define with the same characteristics, since these characteristics had been exactly determined by Hegel.

I return to Hegel, who is a rational reversal of the historical process. No longer is society divided into two parts, one outside the other, which can, at its will, rightly or wrongly, operate on the other, and impose on it circumstances, education, conditions of life at its will. The necessity of rhythm in this organic whole which is society, and which can also be said to be social man, means that the conditions created by one part of society for the other, when two opposing parts of society emerge, are generated from the very bosom of society, which will then reconcile them by itself for the same reason for which it generated them. That is why the philanthropist Owen was a utopian, when he appealed to a feeling of justice to correct the real path of history. Society, by the intimate law of its development, is destined to resolve by itself the contradictions that have been produced within it in its development.

V.

Dialectical Law of Praxis and its Consequences

Everything lies in understanding the concept of praxis, since its dialectical process, just now outlined, derives from its very nature. Praxis is a creative activity, whereby *verum et factum convertuntur*. It is a necessary development, because it proceeds from the nature of the activity, and it comes to rest in the object, the correlate and product of the activity. But this object, which is made by virtue of the subject, is nothing but a copy of the subject, a projection of itself, a *Selbstentfremdung*. The critique of this duplication, its recognition, is an awareness of the subject having been split in two, then synthesized, and, consequently, enlarged. It is not possible, Marx reflects, that the educator has not been educated. Here is the praxis that, by its nature, is inside out. It operates: it fixes itself in an object; it enters into contradiction, which intrinsically resolves itself into a synthesis: educator, educated, educated-educator. Such is the necessary development of praxis.

Thus, when Feuerbach, from his observation of the self-projection of religions, concludes that the religious world is a splitting of the real world, in which it must be resolved, that is, it must be recognized, he does not realize that the inescapable fundamental unity in this duality must be the dialectical spring of a further synthesis. Unity is the real world; duality, produced from unity, presents us with a real world and a religious world, in the bosom of which is hidden the real, which has been denied because it has been overcome. Now the world cannot remain in its negation, because of the contradiction that we allow. Therefore, Marx concludes, the contradiction must be theoretically criticized, and at the same time practically resolved or revolutionized.

The negation of the real world is not resolved with the pure and simple negation of the religious world; it is resolved with the synthesis of the two worlds, that is, with the folding of religiosity on the real world and the *becoming* of this, as it were, with becoming religious. And what is this world? Praxis, in place of perceivable reality. The subject of praxis then, a new Saturn, creates and devours the gods.

And it was natural that this should escape Feuerbach, who, having rejected abstract thought, appealed to sensory intuition; but then he had not conceived of this as practical activity. Hence the usual abstractness: the usual scholastic defect of not conceiving of the two terms (real world, or praxis, and religious world) in their actual relationship.

Thus he reduces the essence of religion precisely to the essence of man; and this essence he understands as an abstract *quid* inherent in the individual. Man, as we have seen, according to Feuerbach, is what he eats. But man eats as a social individual; and to consider his need to eat, and the ways in which he satisfies this need, in and of itself, without considering how they are determined through social circumstances, is always an abstract procedure which can explain nothing of man's life or his history. The essence of man, Marx notes, is determined by the whole of social relations, in which man lives like a fish in water; and since society has a history in which it gradually assumes its concrete forms, man should not be studied, in Feuerbach's manner, as an abstract individual, isolated and outside the historical process, fixing, for example, the religious sentiment as an entity in itself, which is instead concomitant with all the other sentiments of life, and with them connected to the various social relations, according to the various historical periods. But Feuerbach was forced to deny society and therefore history, and to conceive of man as an individual, since he did not have the concept of praxis inherent in sensitive intuition; praxis which alone can explain the organism of society and the becoming of history. This is evident from the things said in the previous chapter; and it will be even more evident from what will be said below.

Note, meanwhile, what other criticism Marx sharply raises regarding Feuerbach's manner of understanding the human essence. Understanding man as an individual, the universal *man*, the human essence cannot be determined otherwise than as a *species*; that is, as the mute universality that binds the many individuals internally by a simple *natural* bond (*blos natürlich*). Beyond the individual, *sic et simpliciter*, there is, in short, nothing but the species, consisting in the natural identity of anatomical and physiological constitutions of discrete individuals; pack identity as the subliminal de facto, which does not value any intrinsic or necessary relationship between individuals.

The basis of society remains purely accidental; like the cosmic structure in atomic theory. Atoms are all similar to each other in quality. But this similarity of theirs would not lead them to conglomerate and form worlds, if there were not, beyond them, something else: emptiness and motion. But the principle of movement is not in them; on the contrary, they are the simple vehicle of movement. And in truth what other intuition, if not mechanics, can help to explain society, when reality is not conceived as praxis, as energy?

Here are two other profound modifications made by Marx to materialism, striving to strip it of its naturalistic character and its mechanistic form. Naturalism wants to explain man as an individual of the natural species, and abstracts from the spirit, or, let us say with Marx, from history, from society. And precisely for this reason, since it admits only individuals, it cannot attribute the origin of society to anything but an accidental fact, such as the consensus and simultaneous deliberation of individuals. It cannot, I say, escape a mechanistic intuition. Let us recall Epicurus the atomist and his concept of the State, imprinted in the axiom λάθε βιώσας[45]; Hobbes, materialist and nominalist (the only reality is individuals, as such), further perpetuated the mechanistic perception of the world and society, as expressed in his social contract theory. It is evident that by reducing man to the pure natural individual, society should be denied, or, just the same, declared accidental. And it is clear that in criticizing this doctrine, Marx comes to deny naturalistic nominalism and the mechanism that follows it, in spite of all their materialism. But will this not be a real and true *deminutio capitis* of the materialistic idea? We shall see.

In the meantime, it is worth noting that, according to Marx, the individual as such is not real; the social individual is real. This is tantamount to affirming the original reality of society, which the individual, the basis of Marx's materialistic view, is pertinent to. Now this is precisely an unavoidable consequence of the first theorem of this philosophy: that reality is praxis. We have seen, in fact, what an intimate relationship binds the subject of praxis to the object, through the concept of this essential praxis to reality; and we have also seen that society is an object, that is, a product of praxis, whereby praxis is reversed and the individual is influenced by the society in which he lives. Now, having admitted the originality of praxis, the individual cannot escape the efficacy of his own product, dissolve himself from the bonds of the society which is the effect of his praxis. Praxis is always the reason for concrete reality; and since it mediates between the individual and society, this and that are as original as it is. The individual, the subject of praxis, makes society, which reacts to the styles of the individual, making him social. This reality, therefore, which is the social individual, beyond which history cannot retreat, is the result of the contradiction that is resolved by the dialectical law of its nature. And without the concept of dialectical praxis, this fact of society, or of social individuals, would not

---

45 *lathe biōsas*: literally "live in obscurity." In other words, to live life quietly and without drawing attention to yourself.

be explained. The earlier materialists clung to the hypothesis of the contract, which, contradictory in itself, is always based on a false nominalistic view. They conceived of individuals in the abstract. The new philosophy once again substitutes the concrete for the abstract.

But in order for this substitution to be possible, what had to be the concept of praxis? This praxis, whereby the individual outside of society and history is an abstract, clearly implies the necessity not only of society, but also of history, indeed of the historical course. The concrete individual of Marx differs from the abstract individual in that it is practical by nature, and yet *necessarily* practical. Now, if the effect of this praxis is society and the historical course, this course is just as necessary as the fact of society; and the study of this praxis, if it is possible *a priori* (and it seems to be, once a dialectical rhythm has been found in it), can serve as a basis for an *a priori* determination of the development of history.

And there is more. This praxis is essentially finalistic; not because it has a regulative, external end, but because it has an internal, constitutive one; that is, one which results from its essential nature. Praxis is the necessary relation of subject to object. Now it is evident that this praxis cannot but be directed to the production of the object; indeed in this production it properly consists. And this production is precisely its *end*. And if this praxis is established in society, in history, then in society and in history there is an immanent objective of development. Each of their forms is the object, the goal of the immanent and original praxis.

VI.

Criticisms and Discussions

This is how the foundations of Marx's philosophy of history, around which the work of interpreters and critics is now more and more troubled, are derived from the heart of his philosophy. The problem is twofold: firstly, did Marx conceive his historical theory as a philosophy of history? Secondly, can one, independently of the actual thought of Marx, support historical materialism with the scope and meaning of a philosophical insight?

These are two different, and distinct, questions. Labriola resolves both in the affirmative; and precisely because his answer is affirmative not only with regard to the second, but also with regard to the first question, it was possible for me in the preceding *Critique* to detect from his writings the characteristics of Marx's historical materialism, considered as a philosophy of history. Benedetto Croce and Georges Sorel, who have not always made the proper distinction between the two questions, answer resolutely "no" to the second question, and also lean towards a negative answer to the first. Alessandro Chiappelli, in his studies of Marx's thought as a historian and interpreter and his research of Marx's historical connection with Hegelianism, has answered affirmatively the first question, but not the second. Moreover, in all his writings Chiappelli has intensely challenged the doctrine of historical materialism.

It is no use now to repeat the reasons why in the thought of Marx and of the communists who followed him (and who actually wanted to oppose the utopians who came before), historical materialism, impetus of the new communist idea, must have been and must be understood as a real philosophy of history.

Nevertheless, allow us a momentary digression, which we will try to make as brief as possible, to consider what Croce and Sorel have written on the subject.

According to the former, historical materialism, in order to be critically acceptable, must be taken as a simple system of historical interpretation that does not "introduce any anticipation of results," but only serves as an aid to seeking them. It is decisively of empirical origin.

This "inexhaustibly suggestive" system must be supported, moreover, by the discernment of the historian, because it cannot always be applied; indeed, sometimes it is completely useless. It is a warning, in short, to the historian that he must be on alert if indeed the facts that he intends to reconstruct in their actual succession of causes and effects do not have their deepest roots in the so-called economic substratum of society. Now I fear that with this interpretation, historical materialism is denied in its essential part. Croce observes that the historian in possession of this system resembles the critic of Dante's text, who in the well-known canon of Karl Witte (i.e., the difficult lesson to be preferred to the easy one) knows that he has a simple instrument "which can be useful in many cases, useless in others, and whose correct and profitable use always depends on his discernment." In this way we come to affirm that the history of human affairs does not always hinge upon that economic life that historical materialism declares the foundation of all human reality. For if always and in every case, history as a whole depended, as Marx wants it to, on the synthetic relations in which the individual lives in society for the necessary satisfaction of his needs—which, as Feuerbach has taught, determine its essence—there could be no case in which the historian would not have to use this instrument.

In order to avoid such a radical consequence, which I do not know if Croce wants to reach, it is necessary to understand historical materialism not as a system similar to that of Witte, useful in many cases and in many others not, but as a system, an instrument to be applied, case by case, always, by those who want to write a realistic history of any social fact. That is to say, not as a specialized system of relative value, but as a general system of absolute value. Otherwise the novelty of materialism vanishes, as it becomes confused with that realism begun in modern history by our Machiavelli.

Now a system of absolute value cannot stand without a philosophy of history that justifies it and is its rational foundation. What does it mean, really, that every historical problem is to be solved by the equation of the fact to an economic x value, with more or less difficulty, based on more or less normalized data, if not that all historical reality has a First on which everything else depends, a unique substance cause of the infinite ways, that in historical development is manifested? And what else is this affirmation if not the core of a philosophical epiphany?

And here is the dilemma: either the system is specialized and relative, and historical materialism can be rejected; or the system is general and absolute, and historical materialism is precisely a philosophy of history. But Croce will not allow us to reduce history to economic reality in order to suit historical materialism, and he will reject the formula we have just mentioned, which smells of metaphysics and monism from a mile away. He notes that the interpretation of Marx's and Engels' genuine ideas is impeded by several very serious difficulties. In the first place, these two authors did not expound their historical doctrine in a book, but:

On the contrary, it is scattered through a series of writings, composed in the course of half a century, at long intervals, where only the most casual mention is made of it, and where it is sometimes merely implied. Anyone who desired to reconcile all the forms with which Marx and Engels have endowed it, would stumble

> *upon contradictory expressions, which would make it impossible for*
> *the careful and methodical interpreter to decide what, on the whole,*
> *historical materialism meant for them.*[46]

In the second place, the special *forma mentis* of Marx—"with which Engels had something in common, partly owing to congeniality, partly owing to imitation or influence"[47]—rejected discussions of concepts, thus sometimes falling into ambiguity and exaggeration; and, thirsting for the knowledge of things, inclined rather to a concrete logic. Hence the double risk of the critics: to make Marx say what he did not think in order to stay too faithfully or too freely to his expressions.

Whereas it seems to me that the exegetical difficulties are somewhat exaggerated, due to a certain idea or prejudice on which Labriola has insisted so much in his essays on historical materialism; and that he puts forward in those expressions we have referred to: *knowledge of things, concrete logic,* and similar metaphorical phrases to which a rigorous meaning is attributed that they cannot have. What does knowledge of things mean? Either this is a metaphorical phrase, to mean knowledge of definite concepts; and this would be a degree, an episode of science, not science proper; or it is taken to mean knowledge of general concepts which are actualized in real life; and then we go from the concrete to the abstract, since we have never seen a general concept among sensible things. So it is with concrete logic. Logic begins, when from the particular, to which real individuals conform, one passes to the general; and the logical concept is its first degree. Go back from the logical concept to the psychological concept or to representation, and you will have passed over the boundaries of logic, to re-enter psychology. Logic then, by its nature, can only be abstract.

But perhaps by expressions of this kind we mean that Marx was an enemy of abstract speculation, that in his knowledge and reasoning he

---

46 Croce, *Historical Materialism,* 78–79.
47 Ibid., 79.

always wanted to move in the field of facts, with the continuous aid of history and experience; and that in this precisely lies the meaning of his opposition to Hegelianism.

Now, I would have some doubts about this definition of his *forma mentis*. On the contrary, it would seem to me that all the productions of his genius demonstrate a speculative tendency that would disgrace any obstinate metaphysician.

In the meantime, here is the field of historical research to which his activity was directed and in which he left the deepest trace of his studies: the history and analysis of economic facts in a capitalist society, with the intention of finding a logical law of their transformation. Now it is Croce himself who, in one of the most valuable paragraphs of the memoir to which we refer, trying to define the scientific problem of *Capital*, writes:

> As regards *method*, Das Kapital *is without doubt an* abstract *investigation; the capitalist society studied by Marx, is not this or that society, historically existing.* . . . *It is an ideal and formal society, deduced from certain hypotheses, which could indeed never have occurred as actual facts in the course of history. It is true that these hypotheses correspond to a great extent to the historical conditions of the modern civilized world; but this, although it may establish the importance and interest of Marx's investigation because the latter helps us to an understanding of the workings of the social organisms which closely concern us, does not alter its nature. Nowhere in the world will Marx's categories be met with as living and real existences, simply because they are abstract categories, which, in order to live must lose some of their qualities and acquire others.*[48]

---

48 Ibid., 50.

All of Marx's writings are philosophical, rather than historical or descriptive. In a letter of his, published by his daughter Eleonora Marx Aveling,[49] Marx wrote from Berlin to his father on November 10th, 1837, when he was nineteen years old and a law student at that university. He revealed that he was inflamed with passionate love for a certain Genny, to whom he dedicated many poems (of which three large notebooks have been preserved, even though he burned many of them!). He was just then ruminating on the long treatises of *Metaphysics of Law*, from which would arise a whole new system of metaphysics, and a philosophical dialogue. Until ultimately persuaded of the inanity of all his arbitrary constructions, he fights with himself, and after studying with renewed zeal and intense ardor philosophy, law, and history, he ends up passing from an idealism nourished by the ideas of Kant and Fichte to the search for the idea in the very bosom of reality; to make of the gods which he had hitherto placed above the earth, the very center of the earth. Thus Marx befriended the philosophy of Hegel, and entered into a circle of Hegelians.

This letter offers the story of his youthful mind, as Marx himself tells it to his father; a story that bodes well for the future enemy of ideas, or ideality, and of abstractions! His *forma mentis* in those early studies is already determined. He will be able to pass from transcendence to immanence, and then from Hegel to Feuerbach—another step, according to him, on the same path. His mind will always be one which, in his first movements, turned to poetry and abstract idealism. He will no longer be able to deviate from the path on which his Semitic speculative tendency has led him. And there is proof of this, as I said, the character of the scientific problem that was formed in his mind, matured and had a solution throughout his life. Because of this tendency, he, having conceived his revolutionary critique of political economy, felt the need to come to terms, as he says in the preface to the *Critique of Political Economy*, "with former philosophical conscience"—to take, in short, a

---

49 *Die Neue Zeit*, October, 1897.

position in philosophy! Because of this tendency he will never be able to resist the temptation to flirt with Hegelian terminology, along with frowning on philosophy, on abstractions! And everyone can see what finesse of speculative analysis there is in the fragments on Feuerbach.

Certainly, the perpetual refrain of these fragments is to replace the abstract with the concrete. But what is the abstract that Marx hunts down? It is the abstract also criticized by Hegel, the basis of the abstract intellect; the abstract in a philosophical sense that contrasts with the vernacular meaning of the word. Normally, the single individuals are separately considered, each one concrete and by itself, as they represent the actual, sensible reality. And these individuals are conceptual to Marx and Hegel. Hegel's abstract intellect is the faculty of immediate understanding, that is to say, which is attached to the details as such, making abstraction from their connection, in which they are concrete. Degree surpassed by philosophical reflection, or speculative thought, which by its nature, does not neglect the details, but raises them in the whole, where they have their connection. The nexus, the general, which for vulgar and scientific reflection is transcendent, in philosophical intuition becomes immanent; and from the abstract it passes to the concrete, transcendence importing nothing but abstractness. What, then, does Marx do by referring every moment from the abstract to the concrete? Nothing more than philosophizing in the Hegelian manner and denying, overcoming it, immediate, positive, empirical cognition—that, if I am not mistaken, to which Croce wanted to allude in his phrase *knowledge of things*. On the contrary, Marx himself, by substituting materialism for idealism, thought of passing from ideas to things, and of opposing, as we see in the fragments on Feuerbach, diametrically to Hegelianism. But we will see in the conclusion of this paper how much reason he had to think so, and what a critic he was of his own doctrine.

One should therefore be more cautious, to take Marx's as a realistic, positive mind—in the most common meaning of these words; not so much to be dismayed when others search at the bottom of his conceptions for a system; nor so much, therefore, to distrust the signification of philosophical phrases that recur in him, so well versed in the terminology of a philosophy, on which his thought was nourished throughout his youth; nor to make him in the end distort what he wanted; and if he wanted to philosophize—since his nature drew him to it—not to pretend that his philosophy is pure dross and not substance of his thought.

Marx's thought was formed and mature, before the cry arose in Germany: *Keine Metaphysik mehr!*[50] before the marvelous naturalistic intuition of Darwinism created in all of Europe that realism or exaggerated positivism, which was the negation of all philosophy, while it certainly promoted the progress of the study of observation, of the *knowledge of things* and of *concrete logic*! It is true, as Labriola points out to the improvised proponents of a Darwinist and Spencerian Marxism, that when the first volume of *Capital* was published (July 25th, 1867), in addition to Darwin's *Origin of Species*, all the main works of Spencer had already been published, and it is also true that at that time the war against all metaphysics was the watchword for almost all of Europe; but since when have the minds of great thinkers taken their shape and direction in old age? We must remember that Marx was born in 1818; and that, time and time again, he is always a Hegelian, formed among Hegelians and always anxious to reattach his doctrines to those of Hegelianism, even if he wanted them to be contrary to them.

No other thinker in our century, outside of the Hegelian circle, has been so anxious to find himself with Hegel! And finally it must be noted that in these fragments on Feuerbach in which there is so much philosophy and metaphysics, one already finds, by the declaration of Engels himself (who certainly had much less sympathy than Marx for metaphysics and Hegelianism), "*der geniale Keim der neuen*

---

50 "No more metaphysics"

Weltanschauung"[51] that is, of all historical materialism, as a general doctrine.

But, Croce observes, the ultimate thought of Engels is that *the dialectic is the rhythm of the development of things, that is, the internal law of things in their development.*

> *This rhythm is not determined* a priori, *and by metaphysical deduction, but is rather observed and gathered* a posteriori, *and only through the repeated observations and verifications that are made of it in various fields of reality, can it be presupposed that all facts develop through negations, and negations of negations.*[52]

Wouldn't this then be a kind of law of evolution? And can the law be said to absolutely dominate things when it is a product of observation? Or is it not rather a provisional generalization, a law of tendency?

It is to be wagered that Marx would give voice this time to his critic, as to another of those philosophers who represent themselves abstractly as subject and object, in that false opposition which we saw criticized above in the first of his fragments on Feuerbach. A law in the philosophy of praxis, when subject and object are conceived in their necessary relation, cannot be determined otherwise than as a law immanent in things. The knowledge we have of things may not be complete; but when we rise from the things we have known to a generalization, which is considered the law of those things, this generalization grasps the essential, the necessary of our knowledge to which things, at this moment of our knowing, conform. So that a law, if it is born in a mind conscious of the demands of logic, must inevitably be drawn as a principle that dominates reality; that if this mind, criticizing itself, realizes that its generalization was a provisional generalization, it means that it will realize that it has not yet achieved adequate knowledge of the thing; that its therefore is not

---

51 "The great seed of the new worldview"
52 Croce, *Historical Materialism*, 83.

a true law, but a provisional stage of its inductive research. And Marx, conscious as he was of the absolute equation between thought and reality, could only conceive of his dialectics metaphysically (whether he knew it or not), that is, as the internal law of things, the immanent in reality. The finding of the so-called laws of tendency is proper to the inductive logic, not to the one that only Marx knew and studied, the Hegelian logic, essentially metaphysical logic.

Now we can accept, if we wish, the rhythm of Marx's economic dialectics as a result of observation, a provisional generalization, a law of tendency; but this much is certain: that he, though he arrived at it by observation—the presupposition of all knowledge—did not understand it and could not understand it, because of the discipline inherent in his mind, except as an absolute law, a necessary rhythm of the intimate substance of reality. He determined it, certainly, *a posteriori*; and how could he otherwise, if this substance of which he claimed to discover the dialectic, was the economic fact, which has, like every other fact, its own history? But he conceived it instead *a priori*; and this is what matters. And in this mixture of *a priori* and *a posteriori*, as I have already believed I have shown, consists the radical vice of his historical conception.

He conceived it *a priori*; that is to say, he believed to discover in contingent reality the absolute reality, which by its own constitution has a real and rational rhythm of development, which revives with the dialectic of the Hegelian Idea.

You must think of the individual essence, Feuerbach had said, as the sum of the material needs of the individual. But this individual, Marx observes, is a social individual, not an isolated one; and his needs, therefore, as material needs, are economic needs. Now this individual, the material subject of the praxis which must satisfy these needs, has an object intimately connected with itself.

And this connection consists in the original praxis which, in producing the object, forms society and history, whereby it is overthrown, and takes place by negation of negation. This procedure of his ends up being an *a posteriori*, and yet it is a true *a priori*. Because there is no history without this praxis; and on the other hand this praxis cannot be rationally understood without that rhythm of development. The dialectic of history cannot therefore but be an *a priori* scheme in Marx's thought. And yet in the author's understanding it not only explains the past and the present; but it must also serve to explain the whole of history, as well as the whole of praxis; and therefore also the future; of which it is not given to mortal man to say anything scientific which is not precisely *a priori*.

And we come to an example. History is a class struggle, according to historical materialism. As Croce writes:

> *I should be inclined to say that history is a class war (1) when there are classes, (2) when they have antagonistic interests, (3) when they are aware of this antagonism, which would give us, in the main, the humorous equivalence that history is a class war only when it is a class war.*[53]

Here, too, I am of the opinion that Marx would protest against such an interpretation of his doctrine: (1) because there is no history, according to him, without classes; (2) because the division into classes brings with it antagonistic interests; (3) because the consciousness of antagonism cannot be lacking where there is antagonism.

Indeed, what is the concept of class struggle in Marx? And the negation of the primitive identity; the non-being of being, in the Hegelian triad. The life of being is in non-being; thus the life of the individual is in society, negation of individuality; and the life of society (all social individuals) is in its negation: in the class struggle. The social man produces; and what does he produce? Capital. Here is the subject on the one hand, and the object on the other: the productive forces on the one hand and the products, the capital on the other; therefore, the

---

53 Ibid., 85.

juridical forms. The praxis is reversed; and the productive forces are modified and grow; and in growing they are in contradiction with the legal forms already fixed with respect to another praxis. But since in praxis lies the indefectible, the necessary reality, development cannot stop; and the class struggle is immediately determined by the conflict between the productive forces and the forms of production, or the law, whatever you want to call it. Hence the class struggle; which, therefore, is the historical aspect of a fundamental and constant fact of life: praxis.

Praxis imports subject and object; therefore, contradiction and conciliation that returns to an ever greater contradiction as a result of the unfolding of the subject. Which by its nature cannot live except in society, and therefore in history. Now the class struggle is bitter; now it is barely felt; now it will not be felt at all; according to the various moments of the dialectical rhythm. In the negation it is barely felt at first and is felt more and more, until it reaches the most serious conflict, when the negation of the negation becomes necessary; for which it begins to diminish until it is no longer felt, to begin again with the previous rhythm, as soon as the conciliation is accomplished. The untiring praxis is the perpetual spring of this descent and ascent of history through the parabola of its development; while social individuals are born and perish, society, the great subject of praxis in history, remains immortal.

The educating society, according to the example of Marx in the fragments on Feuerbach, educates itself; but the educating society and the educated society come into contradiction with each other, and thus the *laudatores temporis acti*[54]; thus the disciples who are rebellious to the masters; the old who do not understand the young; these who turn their backs on them, in order to look to the future. Here is the perpetual contradiction of life. And finally, what happens? The young are always (in general, of course) right over the old; the disciples surpass the masters; and the educating society of the new generation is no longer the same. The practice has remained the same: education; but the new society

---

54 From Horace, meaning "one who praises times past."

educates in a different way; it has other principles of education which do not negate those of the previous society, or do not simply negate them; on the contrary, they negate them by surpassing them, by perfecting them. Society, as educator, has *grown.*

Apply the rhythm of the derived praxis of education to the fundamental praxis of economic life; and it will be understood that, just as the annoying or melancholic admirers of the good old days were never lacking before Horace, nor will they ever be lacking afterwards, so, more or less, the exploiters and the exploited and the consequent class struggle have never been lacking, nor will they ever be lacking—unless a profound revolution of social life takes place.

Therefore, history, i.e. the progressive development of praxis, cannot but produce the division of society into classes, and a correlative antagonism of interests. The exploited are the subject of praxis, the exploiters the object. The exploiters multiply the exploited by the overthrow of praxis. How can one renounce the duality of subject and object? The old abstract materialism, which in fact represented the point of view of bourgeois society, renounced it, or could have done so, because it conceived of the object as a separate entity, independent of the subject; already beautiful and formed, not produced degree by degree by a continuous praxis; so that the subject was reduced to pure passivity, to doing nothing, to being useless at all. This is precisely the concept that the bourgeois has of the proletarian. Everything is in capital, in money; money is money; nor is it understood that capital is the production of the proletarian; that is, that the object is praxis, the continuous work of the subject.

That is why I say that Marx, the opponent and severe critic of intuitionist materialism (*anschauende Materialismus*) or objectivist materialism, would have protested against Croce's interpretation or limitation of his concept of the class struggle, reduced to a simple accidental fact. This interpretation, in fact, can only be founded in the denial or false intelligence of its immanent praxis, the necessary generator of society, history and its eternal contradictions.

Except that, Croce finally objects, if these classes with antagonistic interests are not aware of this antagonism, the struggle cannot possibly break out, and the classes with their opposing interests are not in struggle. But whoever accepts one of the first propositions of historical materialism ("It is not the consciousness of men that determines their existence, but, on the contrary, their social existence determines their consciousness") cannot see in this objection any difficulty. Because, in truth, if this is so, there cannot but be a perfect adjustment between a social class and its conscience: each having its economic needs, to satisfy which it develops that praxis which is doing and knowing together. The way in which each class provides for its own needs is determined in practice, and by so determining itself is determined in thought. So that in the very fact of the division of society into classes of opposing interests lies the reason for the consciousness in which each of them must enter of its own purpose, or, let us say, of its own interests.

Intimately connected with these observations is another subject treated by Croce with his usual acumen in a section entitled: "Of Scientific Knowledge in the Face of Social Problems," the conclusion of which would be purely skeptical: "In face of the future of society, in face of the path to be pursued, we have occasion to say with Faust—Who can say I believe? Who can say I do not believe?"[55] This may be an anguish of men of thought, but the great historical personalities have always distinguished themselves for their great daring, not for an anticipated and scientifically certain vision of the results. In short, it is not possible to deduce a practical program from propositions of pure science; nor therefore from historical materialism. This could coincide with the reported statement of Marx, that not the consciousness of man determines his social being, but this one; since the perfect consciousness of the modern proletariat is determined precisely in science (in historical

---

55 Ibid., 105.

materialism). But the consequence which Croce deduces from this contradicts the materialistic intuition of Marx. The program is not imposed by doctrine; scientific conviction is not enough: it takes historical daring. Thus the first would no longer be the sense, but the intellect, if a strictly scientific proposition were the first operating cause of a practical historical movement. And this would evidently be the most flagrant contradiction into which historical materialism could fall. How? This doctrine, which presumes to explain by the sensible fact (praxis) of the satisfaction of needs, and therefore by the real economic relations which the individual enters into by living socially, all of history, even in its highest and noblest ideologies, must not also explain to us by the same principle this fact in general of our time, which is the theoretical and ethical consciousness of socialism, and singularly the special political movements in which this consciousness develops? Science will be a reflection, an effect, not the cause of practice. Substantial reality lies in praxis, to which then corresponds in the minds of men a special form of consciousness and science; which can, at most, operate on reality by a process of reversed praxis. But the first principle will always be in life, in economic reality.

Now is Croce's skepticism perhaps reconcilable with such an intuition? Absolutely considered, skepticism cannot be grafted onto a metaphysical system; on the contrary, it always presupposes a critique of metaphysical systems. And it has already been demonstrated that Marx's intuition is of a metaphysical nature, as it points to the immanent reality of the various phenomena that history presents to us in its course. In this particular case, then, it is clear that Marx would certainly not have uttered the anxious words of Faust. Belief and non-belief presuppose that absolute opposition between subject and object, which is rightly criticized and rejected by the Trier thinker. When, on the other hand, the object is the work of the subject, doing coincides with knowing; and therefore it can no longer be a question of belief. And if this subject by dialectical necessity of his praxis—in which lies his real life—*must* produce a given object, and is already in on producing it, skepticism is impossible.

According to Marx, the present society has within itself a contradiction, which is the necessary and sufficient reason for the reconciliation of the communistic set-up. Can one remain in this contradiction? No, because the development of praxis is dialectical; nor can praxis stop, because it is the true and only substance of historical reality: the substance that is not and never will be to lack. Nor can there be a shadow of doubt about the course and fact of this praxis, because we are its subject: we ourselves who make history. Science cannot be separated from fact; and now it is not we, opposed to the things that are done, who speak, but it is, so to speak, the things themselves in their making.

We agree with Croce in believing that the abuse of this name of *Science* is enormous. But we must agree that, if there is an unconscious reality, a dialectical practice, of which only a reflection reaches consciousness, it is never possible that a reflection of consciousness—opinion and science—is not the exact correspondent and the translation into intellectual or ideological language of what in fact, in society, is by the very force of things *in fieri*. This seems to me irrefutable, admitted as principle. Nor, if the principle is admitted to be scientifically exact, can the title and degree of science be refused to this socialism which, by virtue of this apodictic affirmation of the future, presumes to oppose all previous communist intuitions, which it defines as utopian.

Not one of Croce's observations therefore seems to me to invalidate my historical interpretation of historical materialism as a philosophy of history.

More briefly, I will be able to deal with a recent writing by Sorel, who, accepting the ideas already discussed by Croce, wanted to research on his own behalf "whether or not the concept of a necessary evolution and a fatal future would result from what Marx wrote."[56]

For Sorel, too, Karl Marx was a "man of action," moved, especially at the beginning, by revolutionary instinct more than by intelligence; one of those men who feel "always great repugnance to analyze their own ideas" and are unable to "clearly establish the distinction between the hypotheses capable of convincing with [sic] what is capable of demonstrating."

But, according to Sorel, Marx is far from being disciplined with philosophical rigor. "More than once he had to let himself go to chimerical hopes," and this is often the case when Marx affirms in a scientific form some social transformation, as if this should follow a necessary law. Sorel agrees with Vandervelde, who in a conference held in Paris for the fiftieth anniversary of the *Manifesto*, said that the three great laws proclaimed by Marx in 1847 had been disproved by experience: the law of bronze wages, the law of capitalist concentration and the law of correlation between political power and economic power. Indeed, he is of the opinion that these statements did not have an absolute value even for Marx, when the words are understood *cum grano salis*.[57] The same can be said of the other law for which in 1850 Marx announced that a new economic and general crisis would trigger a new revolution.

But in the meantime, even Sorel thinks that "Marxists are victims of dialectical illusion and have reasoned like idealists without realizing it." Whereas one should instead reflect on the profound difference that distinguishes the abstract method of the physicist from that of the sociologist. The laws reached by the physicist are objective, independent of our will, of absolute value. The general principles, the dominant characters which are fixed by the sociologist, are instead schemes, reductions of purely subjective value and of simply regulative purpose;

---

56 Georges Sorel, *La necessità e il fatalismo nel marxismo* (Torino: Roux e Frassati, 1898), 3.

57 "With a grain of salt"

because they are useful to the sociologist in his further research, in his applications to particular questions. One should be careful, however, not to take these abstractions and reductions of sociology for "necessary laws of the historical order." Therefore, from time to time it would be necessary to define the purpose for which we make these abstractions and resort to schemes, which are no more and no less than "imaginary correlations" of *sociological reality* "inaccessible to understanding."[58]

These schemes have a purely symbolic value, and are to be understood with a great deal of discretion; formulas of common sense, "indispensable, because science is too abstract to be able to guide action." Such are also the Marxist laws, fixed in a rigorous and systematic way for a pedagogical purpose, to aid the psychological automatism of memory, which always needs these *umbrae idearum*—as Giordano Bruno said, who knew about it—these formulas deprived of a true scientific value, but very appropriate for the practical use, to which they are addressed.

> *It has often been observed that unintelligible dogmas easily provoke heroic acts. It is useless to discuss with people accustomed to lead everything back to great principles, which do not evoke any real image. . . . It would be puerile to condemn processes that have their root in the laws of our mind; but criticism should never confuse the processes of common sense with those of science.*[59]

These considerations must be kept in mind to understand in a genuine way the thought of Marx, whose statements are always subjective reductions, made for pedagogical or propaganda purposes, therefore of relative value and approximate accuracy. Marx's schemes cannot be expected to express "the action of an unknown law that governs the course of history," where they are "summary descriptions, made with

---

58 Ibid., 7.
59 Ibid.

processes of common sense, in view of certain practical conclusions, without any claim to scientific rigidity."

And Sorel then examines some particular points and some formulas of Marxism, in order to prove that we cannot deal, in any case, with necessary determination in the process of historical events.

There is no point in discussing every single interpretation that Sorel, from his own point of view, proposes of the passages he quotes and of the concepts he recalls of Marx. The error of his own point of view is demonstrated by all that has been said above about the speculative tendencies of Marx's mind and his whole philosophy. He, for example, does not want to recognize, with Charles Andler, in that incisive phrase of *The Poverty of Philosophy*—"the windmill gives you society with the feudal lord; the steam-mill, society with the industrial capitalist"[60]—a proof of Marx's historical determinism. This is, he says, an approximate observation. It is evident from the context, that Marx had the simple purpose of showing, thus, wholesale, how to a great transformation of the productive forces corresponds a great transformation in the whole society. Instead:

> [O]ne wanted to find in this simple statement the expression of profound principles, one detached the sentence from the context and wanted to consider it separately as the abstract statement of a great historical law; one said that, in Marx's opinion, the productive forces determine social relations by virtue of a law still unknown, but which science will find later.[61]

The exegetical prudence of Sorel is worthy of the highest praise; but applied as it is to Marx, it only shows that Sorel has remained outside the philosophical spirit of the master. How? Did not Marx write "The mode

---

60 Karl Marx, *The Poverty of Philosophy* trans. H. Quelch (Chicago: Charles H. Kerr & Company, 1896), 119.
61 Sorel, *Necessità e il fatalism.*

of production in material life determines the general character of the social, political and spiritual processes of life,"[62] in that famous place in the preface to the *Critique of Political Economy*, which is quoted by all? And is not this the animating spirit and the intimate essence of the vaunted materialistic conception of history? And is not this general statement exemplified by Marx in the words now quoted from his *Poverty*? Where immediately before he had said: "The social relations are intimately linked attached to the productive forces. In acquiring new productive forces men change their mode of production, and in changing their mode of production, their manner of gaining a living, they change all their social relations."[63]

It will be convenient to interpret the doctrines by declaring part of their utterances as accidental, external, and transient forms, and part real and vital substance. But this must be justified. Thus, it is not enough, *a priori*, to assert that Marx wanted to speak approximately, not with philosophical rigor, when he always took care to start from general premises, and not to apply his analysis to particular cases except to go back to new syntheses of understanding; and he was a philosopher as well as an economist and a historian; and his mind has always shown itself to be impregnated with a strong speculative spirit. Certainly he would have rejected a disciple who had not wanted to admit with him, as a scientific proposition, that the "manner of the production of material life determines first and foremost the social, political and intellectual process of life"; and he had not been able to see in the above example of the mills the typical example of this law.

But "he would have chosen the example very badly," observes Sorel; "the mill moved by arms exists in countries governed by the most diverse systems, and it is very far from being true that it is characteristic of the feudal regime or of any other determined form of civilization." This observation only proves how difficult it is to move from empirical

---

62 Marx, *Contribution to the Critique*, 11.
63 Marx, *Poverty of Philosophy*, 119.

observations to philosophical considerations on history. What does it matter, with respect to the philosophy of history, that in the nineteenth century, back in time, Thomism flourishes again? Not that Scholasticism is a philosophy of modern times, after Bacon and Descartes; but only that there are people who do not understand their own time, deny history, and live in the Middle Ages, even in the nineteenth century. History cannot be said to be at a standstill for this reason; only there are people who leave the main road, turn back, and return to start again on that stretch of road which they did not realize they had taken. In the midst of the capitalist society of the bourgeois century, there is not only the feudal regime, but also the regime—more or less vague—of slavery. What does this mean? That in some countries, by some men, the great path of history has not been kept up. It is said (and who can deny it?) that the French Revolution changed the face of the civilized world. But is it any wonder that in certain regions and in the heads of certain people, after more than a hundred years, none of the great ideas that 1789 proclaimed and wished to realize have penetrated the consciousness of modern peoples? The philosophy of history can only look at the progress of what Hegel called the Spirit of the world—now put into satire, perhaps without being understood—of what Marx would have said the practical matter of the world. What does it matter to him that, e.g., in a large part of Sicily a kind of feudal economic regime is still in force? This does not detract from the fact that in the history of Europe, in which the direct consequences of the French Revolution are evident, the present is the bourgeois and capitalist era.

Nor does it seem to me that Andler was wrong to see in that sentence from *The Poverty of Philosophy* proof of Marx's historical determinism. One must, on the other hand, understand this necessity, according to Sorel's expression, or fatalism of history in Marxism. Usually one conceives of necessity (fatality) as a hypostasis. Usually one conceives of necessity (fatality) as a hypostasis with respect to the succession of phenomena; a superior and external law that regulates the course of things *ab extra*. This is certainly not the thinking of Marx, who, as we have seen, had already passed from transcendence to immanence at the age of nineteen; nor did he go back, indeed he passed from Hegel to Feuerbach precisely in order to replace the abstract with the concrete (according to his way of seeing). Now the necessity of things themselves, the immanent necessity in history, is no longer fatalism, just as it is not really determinism anymore either. Fatalism supposes fate to be superior to men; whereas it is men themselves (not abstract men, but concrete, social men) who make history; nor is there any other energy besides the praxis that is their doing. Society, yes, presses on their doing and gives it a direction; but society itself is a product of their doing.

The question of fatalism in Marx's historical conception had been acutely treated by Stammler in his well-known book, *Economy and Law According to the Materialistic Conception of History*, which Sorel should have known. As early as 1896 this author noted that historical materialism—which he regarded as a philosophy of history—is not at all a fatalistic system. He wrote:

> *The Homeric belief, whereby the goal of life is predetermined for each man, in a fixed and absolute way, without it being possible to lift the veil that covers the inevitable course of events, because it corresponds to the infancy of the intellect, is found at this time among people of the most diverse times and under the most varied circumstances, as well as among Mohammedans devoted to Allah as among men of lower culture in the western countries of Europe. But it has nothing to do with the philosophy of materialism. This philosophy starts from the common principle of causality; it accepts the proposition* non datur fatum, *and is based on the principle that there is no blind natural necessity, but rather conditioned and therefore* intelligible *necessity. . . . It wants to grasp the regular necessity of economic phenomena according to the law of causality and in that to found the universal law of social life. . . . Moreover,*

the materialistic conception of history does not want to be fatalistic in the sense that it wants to accept the law scientifically discovered in the unfolding of economic phenomena as an ineluctable destiny for every single human society, and that it is necessary to undergo without ever breaking down, and against which above all one is not able to give oneself the slightest help. . . .

On the contrary, the materialistic conception of history generally admits that man is able to make the scientifically discovered natural laws useful to his own ends. *And it appeals to the vulgar experience of everyday life; and this possibility of using law* for one's own ends *is held to be so decided that Engels even speaks of a scientifically recognized direction of economic phenomena as a means to a socialistic ordering of society: "It is the leap of mankind from the realm of necessity into that of freedom"; a phrase of excellent external sound, as well as of clear positive content.*[64]

Therefore, no fatalism, but the necessary connection of cause and effect, or rather logical necessity, rational, since the cause to which one thinks is rather the final cause, for that teleologism, which, we observed, is immanent in Marx's dialectics.

Determinism, too, would presuppose an opposition between subject and reality, which Marx does not admit. The principle of all doing, of all history is in man, as matter (the body has to satisfy its physical needs to live); as for Hegel it was in man as thought, in the Idea. Necessity, therefore, in Marx is reconciled, as in Hegel, with freedom, since it comes from the spontaneous development of the original activity, *according to its own nature*. So I would always speak of a necessary dialectic, not of a fatalism of history, according to Marx's conception.

---

64 Rudolf Stammler, *Wirtschaft und Recht Nach der Materialistischen Geschichtsauffassung* (*Economy and Law According to the Materialistic Conception of History*) (Leipzig: Veit, 1896), 38–9.

After all, with a Marxist who writes, "If science is to accept what is scientific in Marx's work, it is necessary to remove from it the contradictions, the false interpretations: it is also necessary to complete and improve it,"[65] we who are here trying to understand and define the genuine thought of Marx have little to discuss. It is useful, however, to point out where this Marxist does not fully grasp the meaning of the doctrine, which he wants to complete and improve; because then it is a matter of interpretation and not of criticism. And in general it may be opportune to observe, for the socialists who toil around the exposition and critical elaboration of Marxism, that Marx's thought is essentially philosophical, and that in order to understand it exactly it is necessary to refer carefully to that Hegelianism which they mock in order to ape the master, often without knowing anything but the caricatures made by him.

---

65 Sorel, *Necessità e il fatalism.*

VII.

Theoretical Marxism and Practical Marxism

Here the question arises: what is, according to Marxism, the position of socialism as political practice in the face of socialism as philosophical conception?

Many socialists, especially in France and Italy, believe themselves obliged to take a stand towards historical materialism, because they belong to the socialist party; induced, perhaps, in this opinion by the fact that Marx was the coryphaeus of the party, and the author together of that doctrine.

But Marx was not a revolutionary, who had recourse to philosophy, only to justify philosophically his own revolutionary theories; but he was also a real philosopher, who by particular studies and by the conditions of the times became a revolutionary. He had been a philosopher before he had been a revolutionary; whereas all ordinary militant socialists are revolutionaries long before they are philosophers, when they take care, when they can, to attain and appropriate this other quality of the master, which is much more difficult to acquire than the first. Now a philosophical doctrine cannot be criticized except philosophically; empirical observations do not touch it.

As to the above duty, we must still briefly return to the concept of praxis as it forms society and history. Historical materialism stands to this praxis as a reflex criticism; as effective as botany which explains how from the flower comes the fruit, it can affect the development of this fruit from the flower. Men make a history, which leads to communism; having reached a certain point, they realize the path that this history is following and the goal towards which, on this path, it is directed. But, whether they realized it or not, this was perfectly useless for the course of this history in itself determined materialistically. That is to say: since the principle of making is not the spirit but matter, which has in itself the law of its development, the progressive implementation of this development is absolutely independent of the determinations of the spirit, even if it is determined by the materialistic conception of history.

But if this is so for one respect, for another, since doing is at the same time knowing, it was necessary that at a certain point of historical praxis correspond the materialistic conception of history; which in fact is, or wants to be, the doctrine of a historical fact that is maturing in the bosom of this capitalist society, in the midst of which it has germinated. And so it is evident that this doctrine, once formulated, which is also a product of praxis, reacts on the subject of praxis, on society, which develops through the process described above of praxis being overturned. Here is therefore the necessity to study and understand exactly historical materialism on the part of socialists, who represent the most energetic and operative part—the most *radical* part—of society, which must move towards communism, in order to solve the contradictions that torment it. Otherwise, the perfect reversal of praxis will not take place, for which it is only possible for its subject to reach a higher degree of development. Society will inevitably change, because contradiction does not allow it to remain in its present state. Meanwhile, we have seen that the class struggle, the spring of change, presupposes the consciousness of the antagonism of interests, and we can also say, the consciousness of historical materialism. And since the class struggle is as necessary as the change in society, the consciousness of historical materialism, that is, the penetration of this doctrine into the active part of society, is inevitable. This doctrine may be misunderstood by one socialist or another; but since it has been formulated, it is impossible that it should not end up dominating minds, enlightening them and holding them up in the great struggle. The sun has appeared on the horizon; and only the barn owls can go and hide in the darkness of the attics: for the others, for everyone, it is light. And historical materialism, by spreading among the pro-letarians its most vital and elementary principles—such as, for example, that of the class struggle—also necessarily contributes to the fatal course of history.

Here is the meaning of Marx's phrase, that the proletarian is the ultimate heir of classical German philosophy. It is always about the overthrow of praxis on the subject; and we know that the new social revolution should be accomplished by the proletariat, which is therefore the subject of praxis.

But, note well, it is only these elementary principles that can react on the proletariat and therefore on history, not the doctrine as such. That reversal of praxis amounts to the negation of negation. That is to say, the object does not return as an object to the subject, but by taking a new form, that is, by becoming subjective; by adapting itself, to put it more plainly, to the minds of the proletariat. So that socialism as propaganda is a mediation between the object and the subject (whence the negation of the negation); it is a quid medium between Marx and the proletariat; in short, it is the disseminator of Marx's thought among the proletariat, adapted to the minds of the proletariat. And yet it is legitimate that socialists, who speak of historical materialism, do not understand it all as Marx understood it; as long as they understand or accept that part of it which they must make penetrate the consciousness of the proletariat, and in it make it powerfully suggestive and operative.

Such is the position of practical socialism towards historical materialism, understood according to the very principles of this.

In the meantime, an objection could be drawn from what has been said above. If praxis is reversed, and ideas operate over history, this materialistic explanation of history itself is not very rigorous. But I have already made this objection on another occasion, when I wrote: "It can be observed that this rigorousness is taken away from the materialistic conception by the conscious agitations of propaganda which seek to hasten the advent of the communist order, and by the moral ideals which true socialist ideas must conform to; ideals which are basically the cause and motive of all propaganda." And already, if I am not mistaken, I think I have shown that Marx and Engels could have replied: Precisely because of the rigorous character of the law that we have found in the overall progress of history, we have enthusiasm of faith, high moral ideals, and we feel strong impulses to work, to prepare or hasten the solution of the social antitheses; and our whole moral being, all the ideologies in which we participate, are a result of the present economic conditions of society.[66] All this receives new and greater light from what has now been observed about the process of praxis. Ideas operate on history, but ideas are themselves a product of the material (economic) reality of history. They are its negation, which must itself be negated and overcome, and the authors of propaganda are but the necessary instruments of such a negation—not unconscious, because the negation of praxis is still praxis, and praxis always means doing and knowing.

And I would like to add that of the two Marxists, Labriola and Sorel, one, in my opinion, is an exact expositor of Marx's thought, the other inexact for being a less philosophical mind than his author, but more practical, I believe, and more open to the individual and determined needs of socialist propaganda. Neither is more Marxist than the other, and neither is in error, from Marx's point of view. Why does Sorel feel that he must improve and complete, as he says, the doctrine of Marx? Because of practical needs, to which there is no doubt that Marx intended to direct all his work. Now it is certain that a philosophical thought, however true, does not represent the content of life and reality, if not in its own form, which is the speculative form of dialectical schemes and categories. Sorel, on the other hand, remaining below philosophy, in the midst of real life, feels, like Croce, that this real life escapes in every way

66 See above, page 33.

from the net with large meshes in which speculative research has wanted to expel it; and it is therefore natural that he also feels the need to *improve*, modify the theory, in order to derive from it a group of directive ideas truly useful to life. That is to say, to return from the philosophical form to the popular form of the content which Marx took to study, to detach himself from philosophy in order to return to life, to break the chain, in order to make some link serve real needs, in everyday politics and in truly effective propaganda. This modification of the doctrine is not against Marx's thought, for if praxis is to overthrow itself, the doctrine must descend to the proletariat, and as a result lose (because of how writers like Sorel carry it out) all its form and philosophical rigor.

But since the negation of the negation is as real as the negation itself in the life of praxis—indeed the reality of the former depends on the reality of the latter—it is clear that Labriola himself is right, with regard to Marx, in always sticking to the philosophical form of historical materialism and by striving to expound Marx's thought with historical fidelity. On the contrary, since this form did not have clarity and lucidity in the work of Marx, who, solicitous also of action, did not have the patience or the time necessary to elaborate the theory completely, it is good and beneficial to the reversal of praxis, that is, to historical materialism as it must then conform in the minds of socialists, that Labriola waits to complete this philosophical form, to finish that essential part of Marx's work, which he could not finish. If the inheritance of the proletariat is a philosophy—which will descend to it by denying itself— let this philosophy mature, so that your proletariat will not find itself with a handful of flies in its hand, instead of with the patrimony which is being extolled!

VIII.

Recent Interpretation of the Philosophy of Praxis

And now let us see how, in his last book, Labriola traces the development of this philosophy.

It seems that he finds the safest and clearest statements in the *Anti-Dühring* of Engels, of which he even translates in the appendix the chapter on the *negation of negation*, in order to explain "in which consists that dialectic which is so often invoked to clarify the intrinsic nature of historical materialism," and by which he intends only to "formulate a rhythm of thought, which reproduces the rhythm of reality that becomes." [67] He frankly recognizes that Engels, in writing this book, "showed excessive disregard for contemporary philosophy, that is, for the *neo-criticism* of his fellow countrymen."[68] He judges, however, that "in socialist literature this remains the unsurpassed book," a book that can serve as a sort of *medicina mentis* for young people who are approaching socialism.

Now it seems to me that in the general outline of this philosophy of Marx's, he looks more to Engels, and especially to the book now cited, than to the more genuine sources of Marx's thought. Nor do I believe, on the other hand, that Engels ever deeply penetrated the philosophical part of the theories of his companion and master.

---

67 Labriola, *Discorrendo di socialismo*, 141.
68 Ibid., 45.

Thinking, says Labriola, is a continuous effort. The empirical matter must offer the means and the external and objective incentives to our thought; but then the mental construction is needed, which from the elementary psychic states rises to the form of the concept and judgment. Thought itself is therefore a work. "There is no doubt that the work done, that is, the thought produced, facilitates new efforts directed to the production of new thought," and we have already noted this above. But the Ego, the subject of this knowledge, is not real if not in a given society, therefore having as its own material and incentive to its construction "the means of social coexistence, which are, on the one hand the conditions and the instruments, and on the other hand the products of collaboration variously specified."[69] The Ego, therefore, is real as part of a "We," of a society, as the term of social relations, which make it gradually grow and become more and more concrete.[70]

This philosophy of praxis (which is *the marrow of historical materialism*) "is," says Labriola, in his drastic language, "philosophy immanent to the things it philosophizes about." Hence "the secret of an assertion of Marx's, which has been for many a puzzle, that he had, that is, reversed Hegel's dialectics: which means, that the rhythmic movement of a thought in itself is replaced by the movement of things, from which the thought is ultimately produced."[71]

Now, I ask, first of all, what does a philosophy immanent to the things on which it philosophizes mean? Philosophy, if it philosophizes about things, cannot actually be *in* things or of things. And to say it is immanent, precisely, to things cannot be said except by metaphor. And so, in the area of metaphor, it does not seem to me that any other philosophy can dispute the same right to say it is immanent in things; at least, no philosophy has ever renounced this claim. And since when one tries to define the special characteristics of historical materialism there is

---

69 Ibid., 55.
70 Ibid., 61.
71 Ibid., 56.

always a tacit and explicit comparison of it to Hegelianism, what philosophy has ever aimed more than this at grasping the intimate essence of reality? The idea, which through nature reaches the spirit and finds its highest form in philosophy, is it not the most substantial reality, indeed the only reality, being therefore nature, things and philosophy together in an inseparable identity? And did not Hegel therefore say in his *Philosophy of Right* that what is rational is real, and what is real is rational? What more intimate interpenetration can be made between things, or reality, and philosophy, than that proclaimed in this proposition, which expresses one of the fundamental principles of Hegelianism? If things are rational, it is clear that a philosophy is immanent in them; that is, that the foundations of their philosophy are in them. And it is strange indeed that this puzzle, even by Labriola, should be understood in the way in which Engels understood or misunderstood it with that very inaccurate knowledge of Hegelian philosophy which I pointed out in his *Anti-Dühring*. I already noted how the Hegelian idea immanent in things was mistaken by Engels for the Platonic idea of its transcendent nature.

And here we hear Labriola speak of a dialectic of Hegel that would be almost "the rhythmic movement of a thought in its own right." But I find that Hegel defined actuality, to which the dialectical rhythm belonged, as "the unity, become immediate, of essence with existence, or of inward with outward," and that he wrote as a comment on this definition:

Actuality and thought (or Idea) are often absurdly opposed. How commonly we hear people saying that, though no objection can be urged against the truth and correctness of a certain thought, there is nothing of the kind to be seen in actuality, or it cannot be actually carried out! People who use such language only prove that they have not properly apprehended the nature either of thought or of actuality. Thought in such a case is, on one hand, the synonym for a subjective conception, plan, intention or the like, just as actuality,

on the other, is made synonymous with external and sensible
existence. This is all very well in common life, where great laxity is
allowed in the categories and the names given to them: and it may
of course happen that e.g. the plan, or so-called idea, say of a certain
method of taxation, is good and advisable in the abstract, but that
nothing of the sort is found in so-called actuality, or could possibly
be carried out under the given conditions. But when the abstract
understanding gets hold of these categories and exaggerates the
distinction they imply into a hard and fast line of contrast, when it
tells us that in this actual world we must knock ideas out of our
heads, it is necessary energetically to protest against these doctrines,
alike in the name of science and of sound reason. For on the one
hand Ideas are not confined to our heads merely, nor is the Idea,
upon the whole, so feeble as to leave the question of its actualization
or non-actualization dependent in our will. The Idea is rather the
absolutely active as well I as actual. And on the other hand actuality
is not so bad and irrational, as purblind or wrong-headed and
muddle-brained would-be reformers imagine. So far is actuality, as
distinguished from mere appearance, and primarily presenting a
unity of inward and outward, from being in contrariety with reason,
that it is rather thoroughly reasonable, and everything which is not
reasonable must on that very ground cease to be held actual. The
same view may be traced in the usages of educated speech, which
declines to give the name of real poet or real statesman to a poet or
a statesman who can do nothing really meritorious or reasonable.[72]

Pardon the long quote. Perhaps it will help to show that Marx, a good
connoisseur of Hegelianism, could not attribute to Hegel a concept of
reality, and of its dialectical rhythm, as Engels and Labriola would like.
Marx could not ignore the fact that Hegel's rational process was

---

72 Hegel, *Logic*, 258–9.

immanent in reality, natural or historical; and the reversal of the dialectic, of which he speaks, must be understood otherwise.

Nor should it be said that the reality that Hegel deals with is the essential reality, whereas the reality of which Marx discovers the immanent philosophy is phenomenal. Let us not charge such a huge blunder to a speculative mind like that of the great revolutionary. He was not so naive as to believe that he could discover or construct an immanent—and therefore essential—philosophy of phenomena as such, just as today we believe we can construct a philosophy of nature by *describing* the phases of its probable evolution. Marx too—it would be good if all communists understood this—was referring to an essential reality, to a reality which is beyond the phenomena; and the things, whose dialectics he said he had found, were not all the things, necessary or accidental, whose infinite phenomenal array history shows us before us; but they were the things in their intimate and, let it be said, metaphysical substance, determined materialistically in economic life. Of course, a great deal of phenomenal reality escapes from the wide net of this metaphysical reality; but that which escapes is not rational, and therefore not true reality, Hegel would have said; it is not economic, and therefore not real reality, Marx would have observed. Therefore he could say that history is essentially materialistic; and what in history is not material, say *ideology* and not *fact*. The reversal that Marx had in mind could be nothing other than the reversal that Feuerbach had made of Hegel's reality; reality, from motionless as it was in Feuerbach, became active, practical in Marx.

We have seen that for Feuerbach and for Marx, the principle of reality is not the idea, as it was for Hegel, but the sensible object. But Feuerbach did not apply to this sensible object the dialectic which had been applied to the Hegelian idea; Marx applied it instead. Whose dialectic therefore stands in relation to that of Hegel in the relationship Feuerbach has with Hegel. Therefore, not abstract thought but concrete things, but Marx substitutes an idealistic metaphysics with a materialistic metaphysics, which must, however, appropriate all the goodness of the latter, the concept of praxis, of the continuous making of reality. This, however, does not mean that we cannot say with Labriola that:

> [*This historical materialism*] *is the end of naturalistic materialism, in the traditional sense of the word until a few years ago. The intellectual revolution, which has led to consider the processes of human history as absolutely objective, is contemporary with and corresponds to that other intellectual revolution which has succeeded in historicizing physical nature. This is no longer, for any thinking man, a fact, which was never* in fieri, *a happening that has never become, an eternal being that does not proceed, and much less the creation of a single time, which is not the* creation *of continuously in action.*[73]

This new philosophy, according to Labriola, also arrives, in the end, at the conclusion of contemporary agnosticism—as much as "*the socialists* would have every reason to believe, that that symptomatic fact (*agnosticism*) is one of the clues of the decadence of the bourgeoisie that it is not given to us to know the thing in itself, the neo-materialists,"[74] in their realistic intuition, without asking for help from the imagination, state with certainty "that we cannot think if not on what we can experience ourselves." This would mean, if I am not mistaken, that the unknowable is a phantom of the imagination, a true *caput mortuum*, as Hegel said of Kant's *thing in itself*; that where there is reality, there it is knowable; that in short, unknowability is always relative to individuals, but there is no absolute unknowability. That was also Hegel's conclusion. But I don't know if Labriola would be willing to accept Hegel's conclusion, since he writes that agnostics "by another way, that is, in their own way . . . come to the same result we come to." Certainly he

---

73 Labriola, *Discorrendo di socialismo*, 57.
74 Ibid., 63.

would not be a faithful interpreter of Marx's thought, if in the quoted sentence he had intended to use the word *experiment* in the Empiricist sense—as Marx, I repeat, was and wanted to be metaphysical.

It is worth recalling Marx's note XI on Feuerbach: "Philosophers have only interpreted the world differently, but the point is to change it." According to Charles Andler:

> *For Marx, it is futile to ask whether thought teaches us what things are in themselves. If we can demonstrate the truth of our thought by giving birth to the phenomena that we have thought, the unknowable, which hides behind, it does not matter anymore. It is not a question of interpreting nature, but of changing it.*[75]

This is evidently the very thought of Labriola, which he wanted to justify with the concept of praxis. Except that in this justification two questions are confused, which one does not have the right to believe were confused by Marx: the question of the certainty of our knowing—a question, as we saw, implied by Marx in the second fragment, and resolved in the way hinted at here by Andler—and the question of the limits of cognition, which are two very different questions. We make things, therefore we know them; because to make is to know and vice versa. But do they arise from phenomena, or from beings-in-themselves? This distinction between phenomena and things in themselves presupposes, as a solution to the problem of the limits of knowledge, precisely that agnosticism which has yet to be presented as Marx's solution, or what should have been Marx's solution. The distinction is foreign to the thought of the Hegelian Marx, who opposes Hegel only to replace the idea, as a principle, with matter, not to change the properties and energy of the principle; indeed, he reproaches Feuerbach and all past materialists for having neglected it. At the meeting, praxis imports an ultra-phenomenal,

---

75 In a review of Labriola's *Essays* in *Revue de metaphys. et de morale* (September 1897): 650.

metaphysical reality, which necessarily transcends those limits of cognition presupposed by Labriola and Andler.

Nor in truth should Labriola come to any other conclusion, who recognizes in historical materialism, if I understand well the long circumlocutions and the cautious if not always precise distinctions, a true and proper *metaphysics*. This metaphysics, at any rate, he insistently contrasts with the *sensu deteriori* metaphysics, against which Engels also polemicized in the *Anti-Dühring*; and which would be marked by these two characters:

> [I]n the first place by fixing, as standing alone and entirely independent of each other, those terms of thought, which in truth are terms only in so far as they represent the points of correlation and transition of a process; and, in the second place, by considering those very terms of thought as a presupposition, an anticipation, or indeed a type or prototype of the poor and semblance of empirical reality.[76]

A kind of mythological formation, concludes Labriola; fixation and hypostasis of what is a simple moment of the real continuous becoming.

But why look for this criticism in Engels, if it is already found in Hegel, or rather, much earlier, in Heraclitus, as Engels himself notes? For it is based on the doctrine of the continuous becoming of the real; whereby every moment is both positive and negative. And Engels, in truth, does no more than repeat, in the footsteps of Marx, the thought of Hegel; from whom, as we noted, Marx borrowed the critique of the abstract intellect proper to vulgar cognition and the particular sciences; an intellect that does not grasp things in their intrinsic nexus, but things in their immediate particularity, difference and opposition. Via Engels:

---

76 Labriola, *Discorrendo di socialismo*, 67, paraphrasing Engels.

In order to understand these details we must detach them from their
natural or historical connection and examine each one separately,
its nature, special causes, effects, etc. This is, primarily, the task of
natural science and historical research.[77]

Here is his own definition of the abstract intellect, of the *trennenden*
Verstand, to which Hegel contrasts the *denkende Geist*, or speculative
thought. Engels himself notes:

*And when this way of looking at things (*Anscauungsweise*) was*
transferred by Bacon and Locke from natural science to philosophy,
it begot the narrow, metaphysical mode of thought peculiar to the
last century.[78]

In short, the metaphysics fought by Engels is the metaphysics fought by
Hegel too, the metaphysics of the empiricists; that is, of those who want
the method of historical and natural sciences to be carried into
philosophy. Metaphysics, therefore, also of modern positivists. And the
metaphysics denied by dialectics; that is, the pre-Hegelian metaphysics.
It is therefore understood that philosophy, which must remain, is also a
metaphysics, in the manner of Hegel.

And this is a point to clarify well. For the metaphysician, says Engels:

He thinks in absolutely irreconcilable antitheses. "His communi-
cation is 'yea, yea; nay, nay'; for whatsoever is more than these
cometh of evil." For him a thing either exists or does not exist; a
thing cannot at the same time be itself and something else. Positive
and negative absolutely exclude one another; cause and effect stand
in a rigid antithesis one to the other.[79]

---

77 Engels, *Socialism*, 78.
78 Ibid., 79.
79 Ibid., 80.

This, at first glance, seems very exact, Engels notes; and indeed he agrees with so-called common sense (*sogenannten gesunden Menschenverstand*). But this common sense, a respectable companion in the home, makes us slip at the first step outside, and drags us into the precipices when we go into the great world of speculative research; it, legitimate in the consideration of isolated facts, as is proper to vulgar or scientific knowledge, beyond these limits becomes "one-sided, restricted, *abstract*, lost in insoluble contradictions."[80] because the particulars prevent us from grasping the whole, the universal in which the particulars live. The trees, Engels says with a beautiful image, prevent one from seeing the forest.

Engels then shows with some apt examples how, everything being a continuous process, these opposites, which common thought conceives to be absolutely opposed, basically unify; and how dialectics is therefore the appropriate mental instrument for grasping reality; the dialectics that opposes the old metaphysics. Everything is both itself and something else. The continuous processes of integration and disintegration of the organism, make the organism at all times itself and other. The cause, in fact, is the effect of another cause, and only by abstraction of common or scientific thought, one thing is a cause, and another effect. Thus, after all, the opposites are as much inseparable as they are opposed; and with all their opposition they interpenetrate each other. And Hegel had already said:

> *Positive and negative are supposed to express an absolute difference.*
> *The two however are at bottom the same: the name of either might*
> *be transferred to the other. Thus, for example, debts and assets are*
> *not two particular, self-subsisting species of property. What is*
> *negative to the debtor, is positive to the creditor. A way to the east*
> *is also a way to the west. . . .*

---

80 Ibid., 80–1.

Instead of speaking by the maxim of Excluded Middle (which is the maxim of abstract understanding) we should rather say: Everything is opposite. Neither in heaven nor in earth, neither in the world of mind nor of nature, is there anywhere such an abstract "Either—or" as the understanding maintains. Whatever exists is concrete, with difference and opposition in itself. The finitude of things will then lie in the want of correspondence between their immediate being, and what they essentially are. Thus, in inorganic nature, the acid is implicitly at the same time the base: in other words, its only being consists in its relation to its other. Hence also the acid is not something that persists quietly in the contrast: it is always in effort to realise what it potentially is. Contradiction is the very moving principle of the world: and it is ridiculous to say that contradiction is unthinkable. The only thing correct in that statement is that contradiction is not the end of the matter, but cancels itself. But contradiction, when cancelled, does not leave abstract identity; for that is itself only one side of the contrariety. The proximate result of opposition (when realized as contradiction) is the Ground, which contains identity as well as difference superseded and deposed to elements in the completer notion.[81]

So, in truth, it does not seem to me that this critique of Engels against the old metaphysics is the great novelty: nor does it therefore have all the value that one seems to want to attribute to it. What is noteworthy, however, is an observation by Engels, later repeated by Labriola, regarding the little awareness of their dialectics that today's supporters of evolutionism have. From Kant, who first argued that Newton's motionless planetary system should be resolved in a process of formation, to Darwin, who gave the coup de grace to the conception of the natural fixed species, there is a whole direction that applies the dialectic to the

---

81 Hegel, *Logic*, 222–3.

natural sciences, in parallel with what was mainly affirmed in philosophy by Hegel. Evolution revives, according to Engels, with Hegelian dialectical development. Everything is in perpetual movement; and the reason for the movement lies in the *coincidentia oppositorum*, which is found in the whole scale of life. But since one can count on one's fingers the naturalists who are experts in dialectical thinking, it is understood that between evolutionary intuition and the method of the abstract intellect with which the results of experience are considered, an insoluble conflict must arise, because of the confusion that reigns in the scientific theories of nature. And is Labriola right to exclaim that "metaphysics, in the sense of what would be the opposite of scientific correctness, is not already a fact precisely so prehistoric as to be on a par with tattooing and anthropophagy!"[82] Just look around us!

Strange, however, is the conclusion that Engels and Labriola claim to draw from all this criticism. "As soon as each special science is bound to make clear its position in the great totality of things and of our knowledge of things, a special science dealing with this totality is superfluous or unnecessary,"[83] says Engels. That would be the conclusion of historical materialism, which, thinking philosophically of reality as history—this being provided only for the individual particular sciences— "he no longer knows what to do," according to Labriola, "with a philosophy above the individual particular sciences." Continuing:

The perfect identification with philosophy, i.e., of critically conscious thought, with the matter of the known, i.e., the complete elimination of the traditional gap between science and philosophy, is a tendency of our time: a tendency, which most often remains a mere desideratum.[84]

---

82 Labriola, *Discorrendo di socialismo.*
83 Engels, *Socialism*, 88–9.
84 Labriola, *Discorrendo di socialismo*, 71.

An admirable example of this identification would be in the mind and writings of Marx, for whom philosophy is precisely in the thing itself; and it is a bad thing that "some vulgarizers of Marxism, who have stripped this doctrine of the philosophy that is immanent to it, to reduce it to a simple *aperçu* of the variation of historical conditions by the variation of economic conditions."[85]

Strange conclusion, I say, because it is drawn precisely from a criticism that had led Hegel to the very opposite conclusion. The defect of the inference derives, in my opinion, from not having sufficiently understood the concept of immanence taken by Hegel. In the quoted passage Hegel says that the result of conciliation is not abstract identity, which is rather one of the two sides of the reconciled contradiction; rather the reason for being, of which identity and difference are necessary moments. This means that being differentiates itself in order to reconcile itself; this is the end of its movement, and it must implement this end, which is its reason for being. Thus the finality of being itself. But if being is final by its nature, it does not, however, carry out the end immediately; that immediacy is the negation of every end. Finality means mediation. Take away mediation, and you have taken away the end.

The tendency, says Labriola, is to overcome the traditional gap between science and philosophy, in the form of a philosophical science, or a scientific philosophy. Very well; but the tendency, the end brings with it mediation (which in dialectics, of course, is not to be taken in its simple chronological meaning); and philosophy therefore can never cease to exist; otherwise, Hegel would say, we would have abstract identity, not reason for being, or rational reality. Contradiction, in short, is not suppressed purely and simply; but is overcome by reaching the identity that is in the very bosom of difference. The difference remains; hence philosophy on the one hand, and science on the other. True identity, full and concrete identity can only live in difference. This dialectical thought unifies giving and having; but not because of this does

---

85 Ibid., 73.

the debtor become a creditor. It unifies being and non-being; but this does not mean that individual things are and are not, according to what we like. Immanence yes, but at the same time transcendence. Pure immanence (understood as simple identity) is a moment of life, of reality, not life and reality. True energy is drawing opposites from the one, finding the point of union, as Giordano Bruno warned three centuries ago. Therefore, the one, yes, but also the opposites.

In fact, if we look at the history of nature, where, according to Engels, dialectics had its proof with Darwin, the human species surpasses and dialectically cancels all the lower species on the biological scale. But what therefore? Is it perhaps that only the human species remained in effect? And the same can be said of each other species with respect to the inferior ones. Thus in history the family is the first nucleus of the State. This is not without it; which, in the State, is not annulled purely and simply, but rather is preserved and is renewed, acquiring its own ethical value, carrying out, that is, its own purpose. The State, says Hegel, is the truth of the family. Thus philosophy is the truth of the particular sciences, and of the products of the abstract intellect in general; just as a science, in which philosophy is immanent, if there ever was one, would be the truth of philosophy.

Rather, I would say that the solution of the contradiction between the particular sciences and philosophy does not lie in a science in which philosophy is immanent, but in a form of philosophy in which the results of the individual sciences are reversed; that is, in a philosophy of nature, in the broadest sense of the term, or rather in what Hegel called a *philosophical encyclopedia*; which does not have to contain the complete exposition of the special sciences and enter into their particulars; but it is enough to indicate their starting point and their fundamental principles; in order to grasp among all of them that intimate connection which escapes the consideration of the abstract intellect, of which the individual sciences are products.—This seems to me the only legitimate consequence of dialectics applied to the productions of the human spirit.

And, setting dialectics aside, it is obvious that the relation of philosophy to the sciences is, for example, that of logic to actual knowledge in general, whether vulgar or scientific. Logic must be immanent in knowledge, in the thought of all; and its origin as an isolated science in its own right necessarily presupposes its immanence in human thought. Now the refinement of this science cannot tend, evidently, to its absorption into the most logically constructed and concatenated knowledge that is possible; but to an ever more rigorous refinement and discipline of scientific methods, preserving, moreover, logic's always independent existence.

Engels himself declares: "That which still survives of all earlier philosophy is the science of thought and its laws—formal logic and dialectics. Everything else is subsumed in the positive science of Nature and history."[86]

Now—apart from formal logic, which I don't know how it can be reconciled with dialectics, while for formal logic contradiction is death, for this one it is the life of thought—what else is dialectics, in the Hegelian way, as Engels understands it, if not that real logic, which according to Hegel contains the whole of philosophy? And in truth, if dialectics is opposed to formal logic, insofar as the latter is the science of the abstract functions of thought, and it is instead the science of things considered in their intrinsic rationality, I do not know how the whole of philosophy and its most substantial part, metaphysics, is not saved from this demolishing criticism. Logic *stricto iure*, and the *general theory of knowledge*, Labriola would say. But whoever looks at the bottom of this general theory of knowledge, must also find in it a general theory of being, if he is a good Marxist and wants to escape the accusation of *scholasticism*, which Marx inflicts on researchers of the way thought reaches being, on those who conceive thought in opposition to being.[87] And I fear that in this way Engels and Labriola only want to fight the philosophy above

---

86 Engels, *Socialism*, 89.
87 See Engels, *Feuerbach*.

things and sciences—*hyperphilosophy*, as Labriola says—understood in the sense of ancient metaphysics. In truth, this philosophy had kicked the bucket a long time ago, long before Marx and the Marxists opened their eyes to the light. Now it is fighting, it is true, with Hartmann's *Unconscious* and Spencer's *Unknowable*; but, look it squarely in the face: it, like the wonderful warrior of the poet, is dead.

"Formal tendency to monism" would be, according to Labriola, the characteristic of this philosophy of praxis; and it would not already be a question of returning to the theosophical intuitions of the totality of the world. "The word tendency expresses precisely the resting of the mind in the persuasion that everything is thinkable as genesis, that the thinkable, indeed, is but genesis, and that genesis has the characteristics of continuity."[88] But this tendency is purely formal; and this implies critical discernment, so that from time to time one feels the need to specify the research, to deny the apriorism of the monistic view, drawing closer to empiricism, and renouncing the "claim to hold in one's hand the universal scheme of all things." All this because of the fundamental principle of praxis, for which to know is to do, and without doing there is no knowing. The form gives rise, therefore, to a monistic intuition *a priori*; but the content of the world, of being, can be drawn only through experience. So *a priori* of the form and empiricism of the content. But does this empiricism of the content limit the monistic view, which one wishes to represent as a simple tendency?

Here, too, we risk confusing a metaphysical question with a question of the critique of knowledge. Is it possible to know what can be experienced without experience? The answer does not come into metaphysics, but into the critique of knowledge; and in fact Kant offers it to us in the *Critique of Pure Reason*: where he says that the category without intuition is empty. Nor have those same metaphysicians to whom you want to oppose you any other way to respond. The same Schelling whom Labriola cites as one of those monists who did not feel

---

88 Labriola, *Discorrendo di socialismo*, 79.

the empiricist requirement, for which the philosophy of praxis would be distinguished from any other monistic intuition, Schelling himself wrote in 1799 in these precise terms:

The assertion that natural science must be able to deduce all its principles a priori *is in a sense understood to mean that natural science must dispense with all experience, and, without any intervention of experience, be able to spin all its principles out of itself; an affirmation so absurd that the very objections to it deserve pity.*—Not only do we know this or that through experience, but we originally know nothing at all except through experience, and by means of experience, *and in this sense the whole of our knowledge consists of the judgments of experience. These judgments become* a priori *principles when we become conscious of them as necessary, and thus every judgment, whatever its content may be, may be raised to that dignity, insofar as the distinction between* a priori *and* a posteriori *judgments is not at all, as many people may have imagined, one originally cleaving to the judgments themselves, but is a distinction made solely* with respect to our knowing, *and the* kind *of our knowledge of these judgments, so that every judgment which is merely historical for me—i.e., a judgment of experience—becomes, notwithstanding, an* a priori *principle as soon as I arrive, whether directly or indirectly, at insight into its internal necessity. Now, however, it must in all cases be possible to recognize every natural phenomenon as absolutely necessary; for, if there is no chance in Nature at all, then likewise no original phenomenon of Nature can be fortuitous; on the contrary, for the very reason that Nature is a system, there must be a necessary connection, in some principle embracing the whole of Nature, for everything that happens or comes to pass in it.—Insight into this internal necessity of all natural phenomena becomes, of course, still more complete, as soon as we reflect that there is no real system which is not, at the same time, an organic whole. For if, in an organic whole, all things mutually bear and support each other, then this organization must have existed as a whole previous to its parts; the whole could not have arisen from the parts, but the parts must have arisen out of the whole. It is not, therefore, that WE KNOW Nature as a priori, but Nature IS a priori; that is, everything individual in it is predetermined by the whole or by the idea of a Nature generally. But if Nature is a priori, then it must be possible to recognize it as something that is a priori, and this is really the meaning of our affirmation.*[89]

Now, I do not see which of these propositions, in which the doctrine of Schellingian apriorism is formulated, can or should be rejected by the supporters of the philosophy of praxis. And this passage quoted one of the most subtle connoisseurs of Hegel, our Bertrando Spaventa, in order to explain to the perpetual and annoying critics of idealistic apriorism, what was the true meaning of *a priori*, on which idealistic philosophy insists, and how for the affirmation of its rights, those of experience were not to be harmed in the least.[90]

Of Hegel it is now said by many that he entirely disclaimed the rights of experience; and they recall the proud judgments he pronounced, in his lectures on the history of philosophy, against the experimental sciences, which, following the example of Newton, *did not make any progress*; and they give him a voice by observing that "Experimentalism, in the footsteps of Galileo and Newton, not only made the already existing sciences advance more and more, but created new ones."[91] If not that a lot of other passages of the works of Hegel could be used in proof of the right value, attributed by this philosopher to the experience; that

---

89 Friedrich Wilhelm Joseph Schelling, *First Outline of a System of the Philosophy of Nature*, trans. Keith R. Peterson (Albany: State University of New York Press, 2004), 198–9.

90 See Bertrando Spaventa, *Studi sull'etica di Hegel* (Napoli, 1869), 42–3.

91 Carlo Cantoni, *Storia compendiata della filosofia* (Milano: Hoepli, 1897), 400.

as proper of the scientific reflection cannot be denied by him if not dialectically, that is preserved and reversed in the philosophical reflection; it would be easy to show how the reproach that Hegel moved to experimentalism was reduced to the reproach that Engels himself moves to it, inasmuch as the purely empirical sciences grasp the single and isolated parts of reality, and not that intimate connection, in which and for which the parts are concrete, and which is revealed to us, as Bruno says, by the *divine art of opposites*, by dialectics.

But I would like to continue with the words of the Spaventa, with his straightforward Hegelian thinking about the relationship of philosophy with experience:

> *It cannot be denied that in recent times the a priori activity has been much abused, and certain constructions of the universe, made almost with closed eyes, with few concepts, or as Hegel would say, with only two colors of the palette, are still famous. But abuse is not a reason to forbid its use; nor has one always seen the activity of speculative thought proceeding in a vacuum, without taking into account facts, history, real life, nature and spirit; and someone has given us back the image of Aristotle, whose sharp and sure eye penetrated into reality and discovered its innermost essence in thought. The cause of the same abuse was the novelty of the concept, so essential to modern philosophy, of the infinite power of knowing; which filled and moved the spirits and gave them immense and almost youthful boldness. Certainly without experience one cannot have any knowledge of things. But what experience does not give, nor can it give, is the nexus, the relation or the system of all things. This system, in which true reality consists—since no thing is real except in the universal system of things—is . . . the object of philosophy. The data of experience are multiple, loose, isolated, disconnected, and receive unity—and therefore true meaning— only from speculative thought. And in this—in this relation with*

experience—consists the originality *(priority) of thought; since nothing but thought is and can be that unity in which alone all things are real. Therefore, experience is not the reason for thought, as it seems at first sight and is commonly judged, but rather it is the reason for thought. Experience is only the temporary basis—the negative starting point—of thought; which therefore presupposes it, but does not draw from it its authority, its light or evidence, but from itself alone: from its own relations and terminations. And in fact, since thought is essentially unity, relation, connection, and since this connection is not given by experience, light and evidence can only arise from thought: it is thought itself.*[92]

Another time Labriola wrote: "We must hope that philosophers like Krug, who explained the pen with which he wrote by a process of dialectic deduction, have remained forever buried in the notes of Hegel's logic."[93] But Guglielmo Krug was no less an enemy of *a priori* constructions than Labriola, because he was a Kantian, and he did not deduce from the pen; rather, he challenged Schelling to the arduous task, thus demonstrating that he had not understood in what sense Schelling supported the apriority of nature. And allow me just one more quotation from Spaventa himself—whose books I do not know why people do not want to read anymore in Italy:

This fear, this horror against the proof of creation (that is, the a priori *construction of nature), is nothing but a misunderstanding. To prove creation is not to prove the contingent as contingent, this or that contingent; for example, that such or such a stone, such or such a plant, etc., must be there. Krug demanded this from Schelling. Schelling said: I must construct nature a priori; and Krug: construct for me the pen, this pen with which I write. Schelling meant to say:*

---

92 Bertrando Spaventa, *Principii di filosofia* (Napoli: Ghio, 1867), 96–7.
93 Labriola, *Essays*, 219.

> *Nature, true Nature, the idea of nature is a priori, and precisely*
> *because it is a priori, it can be constructed a priori [according to*
> *what is shown in the passage of Schelling himself just referred to].*[94]

But, apart from this and some other *telum sine ictu*, it is certain, if the documents adduced suffice, that the historical materialists do not succeed in a monism which differs in anything from the monism of the idealists, whom they believe they have overcome forever, because of the experimental requirement which they affirm; and their intuition is monistic not only as a *tendency*, but also *essentially*. And monism is not only of form, but also of substance. Since there are two kinds of monisms: that monism of Leibniz, with its infinite monads, because all these monads are metaphysical points and centers of force, and one is therefore the form of the universal reality; on the other hand there is the monism of Spinoza, for which the *substance*, despite the insurmountable duality of the attributes (*form*), is metaphysically unique. Here is an example of pluralism that is at the same time monism, and an example of monism that is at the same time dualism, according to whether in order to define the system one looks at the way in which the substance itself is conceived, or at the way in which the form of the substance is conceived. Absolute idealism and historical materialism are indeed two monisms, both of form and substance. Everything is in continuous becoming: monism of form. Everything is essentially an idea, or everything is essentially sensible reality, matter: monism of substance.

Nevertheless, Labriola does not declare a tendency to formal monism, but a "tendency (formal) to monism," even though the monistic character of the philosophy of praxis only consists in the notion of becoming, that is in the *form*, not in the substance of metaphysical reality.

Formalism applied to *tendency* is somewhat of a misnomer, but it hints at that necessary immanence of philosophy in science, of which

---

94 Bertrando Spaventa, *Prolusione e introduzione alle Lez. di filosophia nella Università di Napoli* (Napoli: Vitale, 1862), 183.

historical materialism is deeply aware. Only because of the formal character of our scientific progress do we tend toward a monistic conception of everything as continuous praxis and perpetual becoming. We must allow ourselves to be led by this common thread, by this fundamental norm in individual and specific scientific research: by the concept that everything becomes. But this concept must not itself become the object of special consideration or research, thus becoming, itself, the object and content of thought; for in that case our tendency to monism would no longer be formal, that is, it would no longer touch only the form of our scientific knowledge, but also its content, and would give rise once again to that philosophy per se, or hyper-philosophy, which historical materialism has the merit of denying, affirming the "realistic need to consider the terms of thought, not as fixed things and entities, but as *functions*."[95]

By now this point has been made quite clear. That the categories of thought are not to be considered as fixed entities, preformations, but as functions, has for a while been established within philosophy, since the *Critique of Pure Reason*, though for a long time this idea was misunderstood by many philosophers and critics of Kant. Nor had this understanding of the categories as functions in place of knowledge, and in themselves quite empty, escaped the builders of the new metaphysics. But, as Hegel asked, empty of what? Of empirical content; and this is precisely the requirement of speculative thought, which must not linger in diversity (in the concrete determinations of experience), but ascend to the universal, to identity. It is not a defect for philosophy, Hegel noted, to deal with these abstractions, which are categories themselves empty of empirical content; indeed, it is its merit, its perfection.

A glimpse of this meaning of content may be observed to affect our ordinary thinking. A book or a speech for example is said to have a great deal in it, to be full of content, in proportion to the greater

---

95 Labriola, *Discorrendo di socialismo*, 65.

number of thoughts and general results to be found in it: whilst, on the contrary, we should never say that any book, e.g. novel, had much in it, because it included a great number of single incidents, situations, and the like. Even the popular voice thus recognizes that something more than the facts of sense is needed to make a work pregnant with matter.[96]

And yet I have once again distinguished, in order to harmonize Kant with Kant, and Rosmini with Rosmini, the category as such from the category as concept; a very useful distinction to understand the rights and the legitimacy of the new metaphysics, which is *logical* by its nature.[97]

It should be noted that the category as such is not conceivable, for that same reason for which Aristotle claimed that matter and form make an inseparable whole, a sinòlo.[98] Kant warns: the category is what it is, as it has the content provided to it from perceptible observation; without this insight it is empty. Thinking means judging, and judgment is the necessary synthesis of category and empirical content. Outside this synthesis there is no thought. How is it, then, that in the *Analitica dei concetti* he speaks of these *reine Begriffe*, these pure categories, empty of all content? Or how can one speak and deal scientifically with what is by its nature unthinkable?

Certainly, the category as a function of thinking is not thinkable except as a function, that is, together with the content, with the sensible datum, which it serves to form. But insofar as we say that it is thinkable only as a function, together with the sensible content, do we not *ipso facto* construct the (abstract) concept of this function? Now it is precisely the concept-category, not the category as such, the category that logic deals with, which in a philosophy that identifies being with thought (or as idea,

---

96 Hegel, *Logic*, 91.
97 See Gentile, *Rosmini e Gioberti*.
98 From σύνολον, an Aristotelian term that designates concrete substance, conceived as a synthesis of matter (mere power) and form (that which brings the potentiality of matter into action).

or as sensible praxis), assumes the dignity of metaphysics or philosophy properly so called.

The category as such is in the fact; the category-concept is in *science*. The fact is the object and the logical presupposition of science; it is not science itself. Thus, the category is a function which is implemented (therefore nothing independent and per se) in the fact of concrete knowledge; but if we want to subsume this category in science, if we want to know and study it, it is not possible for it not to become concept, and therefore not to be fixed as per se.

Woe to science, if it were forbidden this perpetual abstracting process! And in what else, in fact, does that Socratic moment of every form of knowledge consist, of which Labriola so rightly points out the importance? To form concepts or to elaborate them (Herbart) is to transcend the particular, the concrete, and to rise to the universal, to the abstract. In the anxieties of the empirical individual there is no concept whatsoever. And we cannot depart from individuals except by abstraction. Nor, on the other hand, is there science without the elaboration of concepts, without Socratism. Science therefore inescapably wants, as its own raison d'être, the abstraction and hypostasis of the abstract—not as concrete, however, but as abstract— which is equivalent to what is more commonly called the formation of concepts. Thus the new logic cannot treat the categories as functions of thought otherwise than as terms, as objects of thought itself, that is, as concepts. And yet I conclude, that there can be no merely formal tendency to monism, if this tendency is to mean a philosophical habit, a reflection, and therefore a knowledge however initial. Nor, on the other hand, is it to be believed that, coming out of the specified research, and constructing a true and proper philosophy, we must at all costs deny or forget that the categories, on which it will work, will not be, in the real fact of our knowing, if not pure functions of this knowing itself.

The ideal of this new philosophy of Labriola would be *Capital*, where philosophical thought and positive knowledge of economics, history, and law make an inseparable unity, scientific thought in the most perfect philosophical awareness. Certainly the scholars, the researchers of themes by profession, as they have collected Dante's geology and Shakespeare's entomology, "so *a fortiori*, and more rightly, they could write about the logic of *Capital*, indeed build a whole of Marx's philosophy, etc."[99] But *Capital* lives in its *elusive* integrity.

If not that, only this work represents a group of knowledge, which make an organic whole, not analyzable, without ceasing to be what it is; or is this proper to all knowledge in general, and to every part of life? When one recognizes the raison d'être of logic, does one not already admit that the scientific spirit can analyze every synthesis of life? Logic is immanent in the common knowledge of man; but it is not born as a science, except when it begins the analysis of what is in fact inseparable.

Or go, pray, to anatomy, without destroying with your knife the whole of the corporeal organism. It is enough for logic to be aware of its abstract or transcendental character; it is enough for anatomy to conceive the inert arm detached from the torso as a part of a living organism, so that science respects the rights of reality, always organic by nature. And Marx knew that in his capital work he continued, as Croce clarified, an abstract research.

As for the philosophy of *Capital*, the right to look for it within comes from recognizing its immanence. And Marx was perfectly convinced of this, too, as he gave himself the thought of coming to terms with the philosophy of his time; of philosophically justifying his own revolutionary historical-economic theory; of seeing a little, in short, what philosophy was immanent, precisely, in his thought.

"It is a matter of taste," finally exclaims Labriola. No—a materialist like Marx cannot reduce the facts of history of this importance, such as the great analytical manifestations of the human spirit, to a question of taste, for Marx's materialism sees nothing accidental in history. And if the human spirit is so made that it always transcends organic reality by

---

99 Labriola, *Discorrendo di socialismo*, 77.

the power of its analysis, no one will be able to dictate laws to it that are not in keeping with its nature.

On the other hand, it is so unlikely that Labriola, in the meantime, is writing about philosophy transcending any specific research; and he is waiting to clarify this philosophy of praxis. It is indeed true that philosophy is *form* not mental *content*, and if it has its own content—as it certainly does—this is the transcendental hypostasis of form; but with this is formulated what is true in the whole critique. This concept seems to us of capital importance.

Finally, since historical materialism is also a metaphysics, is it optimistic or pessimistic? This too is a question often debated, and Labriola does not let it slip. As was to be expected, his solution does not differ from the Hegelian one.

> *Optimism and pessimism, in the sum, consist in generalizing the affections resulting from a certain experience or social situation, and in prolonging them so much outside the sphere of our life, as to make them the axis, the fulcrum, or the purpose of the Universe.*[100]

So that the categories of good and evil, purely relative in their nature, become absolute principles of life, and its teleological causes; where in reality they are nothing but simple ideologies. Now "historical materialism, as the *philosophy of life,* and not of its ideological appearances, surpasses the antithesis of optimism and pessimism; because it surpasses their terms by understanding them." This painful path of history, which can be called the *tragedy of work*—a tragedy that was not avoidable, because it does not derive from caprice or sin, but from a necessity intrinsic to the very mechanism of social living—leads itself to "the means necessary for *its perfection,* first of a very few, then of a few, then of more than a few—and now it seems to prepare some for everyone." Once the evil of the slaves was the good of the masters; then

---

100 Ibid.

the evil of the vassals was the good of the lords; then the evil of the proletarians was the good of the capitalists. A time will come when this contradiction of the evil that is good, and of the good that is evil, will be resolved into the good of all, which, however, not opposing evil, will no longer be truly good, but the unity of good and evil. But the triumph of communism will not already be the work of *eternal justice*. "That beneficent lady will not move a single one of the stones of the capitalist edifice." In the present evil the materialists find precisely the springs of the future; and this they expect from the rebellion of the oppressed, not from the goodness of the oppressors.

What does all this mean? That what is, must be; the real is essentially rational, just as Hegel said. The opposition of good and evil will remain a contradiction of the abstract intellect, which speculative thought resolves, overcoming it, like any other contradiction. Good and evil do not exist in essential reality; but, as Marx says, they are ideologies. Historical materialism and Hegelianism in the same way, therefore, surpass in theory the pessimistic and the optimistic point of view. But in fact they are both purely optimistic systems. What is must be; reality is rational. But in the meantime, this reality, as history, represents the fatal journey of the World Spirit towards the freedom of all, in Hegel; or the ascension of man "from the immediacy of living (animal) to perfect freedom (which is communism)," in Marx. In history there is therefore a finality, since every step is aimed at a goal, and this finality is essentially optimal. And since finality is immanent in the historical process from its first beginning, like Hegelian intuition, Marxist intuition is in fact optimistic, contemplating a history that walks towards an end, which is the good of all, the absolute good.

IX.

Critique of the Philosophy of Praxis

From critics and interpreters, returning now to Marx, from whom, moreover, we have never strayed even in apparent digressions, and summing up, we can define the philosophy of praxis outlined by Marx in the fragments of 1845, as a materialistic monism, which is distinguished from any other similar system by the concept of praxis applied to matter.

But how does Marx understand his matter? As praxis, one replies: from historical materialism. That is to say, a system which does not conceive of matter as fixed and stable, but as continually becoming. But where is the principle of activity? In Marx, praxis is synonymous with *human sensory activity (menschliche sinnliche Tätigkeit)*. Therefore, the activity of matter resides in man. Sensibility is precisely the practical activity; human-sensitive activity. Hegel said that the idea, the spirit is industrious; and that its dialectical development is the reason for the becoming of reality. Marx does nothing more than substitute the body for the spirit, the idea for the sense: and to the products of the spirit, in which for Hegel true reality consisted (and which for Marx became ideologies), the economic facts, which are the products of human sensory activity, in the search for the satisfaction of all those material needs, to which Feuerbach had reduced the essence of man: but he preserves all the rest of the Hegelian conception. And the substitution of the body for the spirit, of the sense for the idea, was natural and necessary: Feuerbach himself had done it. Since the first degree of phenomenology is the sensitive consciousness, or sense as it may be called, and from it all the higher degrees then develop, it is the true activity of man. To it must be attributed the rights usurped by abstract thought.

So others might say that since man derives from the child, it is not man who works and wars and does science etc., but the child, in the last instance. If he were invited to point out to us the miraculous child, he would perhaps find himself in a great embarrassment; no greater, moreover, than that in which Marx finds himself in proving that sense is truly the principle of reality, understood as he understands it.

Who can deny any more that our sensory activity is the true demiurge of sensible reality? The vibration of the ether does not appear to the eyes, but the color does; and the color is therefore the *sensible* reality. Now it is clear that this reality is not *given* to the senses, because outside of us there is nothing but etheric vibration; it is produced by the senses. Except that, just as the Platonic demiurge does not create *ex nihilo*, but has before him and opposite him matter, which he molds into the various sensible forms in imitation of the eternal ideas, so sense does not create color; but the external datum (ethereal vibration) it transforms into visual sensation. The datum alone is anything but sensation; but sensation is impossible without the datum. Now then: who provides this datum? Psychology answers: the external world; and this answer is sufficient for psychology. But when Marx opposes his senses, his body, his matter, to the idea and the spirit of Hegel, it is no longer a question of psychology or phenomenology, but of something else: it is a question of logic, according to Hegel's wording; that is, of metaphysics. And so also psychologically it can be said that the sense creates the sensation, because psychologically beyond the color there is nothing, and the ethereal vibrations are a purely physical fact. But when from the particular consideration of psychic phenomena we pass to the general consideration of reality, we see immediately that beyond and before color, there is the vibration of the ether. And who makes the vibrations? God, replies the spiritualist; Matter, replies the materialist. But it is evident that this matter is beyond the scope of human sensory activity, which should, according to Marx, shape and construct it in its own way. A scholastic question, Marx would say: the etheric vibrations, as such, are a pure abstract, something that does not exist (with respect to man). Ethereal vibrations do not exist apart from color. Except that this answer makes us fall once again into phenomenology, while it is the Hegelian Logic that the author intends to oppose, and it is the metaphysical materialism that he believes to correct with his dynamic concept of matter. And in this field the *relative* must give way to the absolute, as the *a posteriori* becomes *a priori*.

In idealism this process of the *a posteriori* to the *a priori*, with respect to the universal reality and the absolute, is understood. Knowledge, said Kant, is made up of synthetic judgments a priori; that is, experience (synthesis) that is posed, fixed and recognized as a priori. The category, the original function of my intellect, must be offered the datum of sensitive experience, so that the concept is formed. The genesis of every concept is necessarily empirical, *a posteriori*. But, once formed a universal concept, a law, this concept, this law are a priori, and dominate, as such, reality. Now, if one does not arrive at the universality of the law, of the concept, and remains in the particular of sensitive intuition, it is evident that one does not leave the *a posteriori*, that is, the field in which one finds only what is given by experience: and sensitive experience always supposes the stimulus, as its indefectible antecedent, and, for it, matter. Matter therefore escapes the creative activity of the sense, nor can it receive a norm from it; on the contrary, it influences it and dictates to it in some way (the varying speed, for example, of ethereal vibrations produces the diversity of colors).

Idealism observes that concepts and rational laws dominate reality; and thus there are no chemical bodies which are not subject to the mathematical relations of their formulas, nor is there a wolf or a horse which is not a quadruped or a mammal, according to the necessary notes fixed by zoology, nor is there any water which does not freeze when it descends to a certain temperature, according to a law known by experience. Therefore reality itself is as if constructed by reason, which appears immanent in it; and reality, therefore, is essentially rational. Certainly the reason to which reality is adapted cannot be that of Hegel, and even less so my own, or that of Titius or Caius. But this is important to note: that all of nature is written in mathematical characters, and that the mind can read these characters; or rather that these characters, insofar as they are mathematical, are by their nature mental or intelligible, mathematics being nothing but constructions of the intellect. The mathematics of nature is precisely its rationality; or the reason or idea, as it were, that is immanent in it and in reality in general.

The passage, therefore, from *a posteriori* to *a priori*, as the reason for reality, is understood in idealism; but in Marx's materialism it is inconceivable.

The only way out would be for it to deny everything that transcends sensory reality; and this would be the genuine character of materialism. But the very affirmation of this sensory reality as pure and simple matter immediately transcends sense.

And, on the other hand, if nothing is real which is not sensible and material, all that criticism which Marx makes of the earlier materialistic conceptions of society, undoubtedly ruins. He is opposed, as we have seen, to the nominalist intuition which sees in society nothing but individuals, who may agree with each other, but who are always essentially independent of each other and on their own; and he rightly observes that this is an abstraction, because society is original, and individuals, therefore, are nothing but organically connected parts of a single whole. Now then, what is there of perceptible reality in society apart from individuals as such? Their organism, society, is an ethical bond, it is mind, rationality; and not for nothing, therefore, did the subsequent materialists, such as Epicurus, Hobbes, and the French materialists of the last century, deny society as a necessary and original fact. Organism and society imply relation: and relation is not touched, nor seen, nor heard: only its terms are sensitive. If you conceive the terms with their relation, you ascend from the sense to the intellect, not by denying the sense, but by making an *a priori*, or necessary, synthesis of it and the intellect.

Meanwhile Marx had a reason for not isolating individuals, abstracting them from their relationships. This reason, as we have made clear, was in the concept of praxis, immanent in sensible reality. Praxis means the relationship between subject and object. So neither individual-subject nor individual-object, as such *sic et simpliciter*; but the one in necessary relation to the other, and vice versa. So again, the identity of opposites. Not educators on one side, as we have said, and educated on the other: but educators who are educated, and educated who educate.

Thus we have seen Marx drawn from the very concept of praxis to deny naturalism. And Labriola says well in the spirit of his master, that:

> All men who live at this moment on the earth's surface and all those who, having lived in the past, were the objects of any trustworthy observation, are found, and were found, already sufficiently removed from the moment when purely animal life had ceased.[101]

This denial of naturalism is another blow to the materialistic doctrine, that there is nothing but sensible reality; because *purely animal life* is the living precisely of sense and among sensible things; and it does not cease, if not with the affirmation of something more than pure sense. The moment, in fact, in which it ceases, the moment to which Labriola himself refers, is the moment of the origin of society, and, as we have already said, the affirmation of mentality (for which sense is already overcome).

Materialism cannot see in man anything other than the animal (naturalism); but Marx, by virtue of his concept of praxis, is forced to see

---

101 Labriola, *Essays*, 115–6.

in man something more than the pure animal, to see in him man, that is to say, the animal, but the animal by its political nature, according to the old Aristotelian expression.

But what kind of materialism is this? Like all materialism, it does not want to recognize as real anything but what is perceptible, but this perceptibility, which is static for all other materialism, is dynamic, for it is perpetually *in fieri*; hence its appellation of historical materialism. And here this materialism, to be historical, is forced to deny in its speculative construction its own foundation: that there is no other reality apart from the sensible; and thus to reject the essential characteristics of every materialistic intuition: such as, for example, the atomistic conception of society, and naturalism itself. This, in short, is a materialism that to be historical is no longer materialism. An intrinsic, profound, and irremediable contradiction troubles it.

And in truth, had not Hegel said that the spirit is history? The spirit, not matter. Can history, as Marx claimed, be transported from spirit to matter? The materialism of the last century, which was in fact the sincere expression of the anti-historical century par excellence, did not believe so, and it had its good reasons. Because that materialism understood matter as such; and matter as such is always identical with itself, it never changes. Its forms differ, and these change and vary indefinitely; but it remains constantly the same in all its forms. So from a piece of clay, first make a jar; then, after reshuffling it, you can make a bottle out of it; but, jar or bottle, clay is always clay; and as such, it cannot be said to change. And where there is no change, there is no history. If you then want to look at its different forms, you no longer have before you clay pure and simple: but clay and the shaping hand, clay and praxis. And so, if you want to look at matter not in itself, but in its ever-varying forms, that is, in its history, you will have matter and praxis which makes it be in all its forms. But if you accept praxis, you transcend, as we have seen, sensible reality. Nor did the materialists of the last century want to transcend it; they were therefore content with matter as such, always identical with itself, without history. Hence their conviction that the world has been and always will be the same, and that in order to know any being intimately, one must not study it in its history, but in its natural state. Hence also that return to nature, which is the character of every production of the thought of the last century; even of political economy, with the Physiocrats.[102]

Applied to the law, one can understand how the intuition of the philosophers of the eighteenth century could lend itself to revolutionary doctrines that would prepare the outbreak of the great revolution. Because, in fact, a revolution is a denial of history, a denial of the value of what history has consecrated as the natural movement and development of human society; treating historical facts as accidental modifications—and therefore changeable at will—of nature, eternally identical with itself. In historical materialism, however, the aim is to proclaim that history is the only real mistress of us all, and that we are as it were *lived* by history, as Labriola says. Then it is affirmed as the canon of the new philosophy that, if philosophers have so far only tried to *interpret* the world, now it is a matter of *changing* it (*verändern*); that is, of changing history, in which, for the new materialists, every reality consists. That is to say, that this unique reality, which is history, whose essence is determined by dialectically necessary development, suddenly becomes unreal, by the very fact that its development must stop, or change course. And in what way, or why? By the speculations of philosophers! More than historical materialism! Those much-derided ideologies would suddenly become the wellspring of history! Because, in truth, the philosophers have no other means than philosophy, at their disposal, to change the world.

Do we not thus return to the Platonic view of the ideas as the motive and creative forces of the universal reality?

---

102 The Physiocrats were a school of economists in France. They may be seen as some of the foundations of liberalism. They taught that wealth derives from labor. They already advocated for laissez-faire economics and philosophical individualism. Adam Smith even met the Physiocrats including Turgot when he went to France.

The root of the contradiction, which crops up at every turn in Marx's materialism, lies in the absolute lack of any criticism of the concept of praxis applied to sensible reality, or to matter, which are equivalent for him. Marx does not seem to have taken the slightest care to see how praxis could be joined with matter, as the only reality; even though the whole preceding history of philosophy must have warned him of the irreconcilability of the two principles: of that form (praxis) with that content (matter).

Matter itself is inert, therefore always equal to itself. From where does it derives its industriousness, its incessant becoming-of-itself? It can also be said that a force is immanent in it; but this force, which gradually transforms matter according to a dialectical and finalistic development, is a rational force: it is reason, it is spirit. And so the spirit always presents itself as original, beyond matter; and, as well as concluding with a materialistic monism, one succeeds in a more or less Platonic dualism. The outspoken materialists contemporary with Marx himself, such as Büchner, clung to the faction that acknowledged force and matter as original, but they took care to keep away from force every finalistic view; on the contrary they worked on an inexorable criticism of every teleologism, as of one of the fundamental theories (now vigorously reaffirmed by the idealistic English and Americans) of idealism.

Karl Marx, a born idealist, and who had been so familiar, in the formative period of his mind, with the philosophies of Fichte first and then of Hegel, did not approach the materialism of Feuerbach forgetting all that he had learned, and that was ingrained in his thought. He was not able to forget that there is no object without a subject that constructs it; nor was he able to forget that everything is in perpetual *fieri*, everything is history. He learned that this subject is not spirit, ideal activity, but sense, material activity, and this all (which always becomes) is not the spirit, the idea, but the matter. In this way he believed he was proceeding along that path along which he had set out, passing from Kant and Fichte to Hegel, almost from an idealistic transcendence to an immanence; in this way he presumed to move further and further away from the abstract by approaching the concrete. But in the question of abstract and concrete, how can we not take into account the stupendous Hegelian critique of the abstract intellect? So matter yes, but matter and praxis (that is, subjective object); matter yes, but matter in continuous becoming. In this way he came to grasp "the most beautiful flower" of idealism and materialism; the flower of concrete reality and of concrete conceptions always substituted for abstractions, and of Hegel and Feuerbach. Materialism yes, but historical. Except that the irony of logic responded to the excellent realist intentions with a result that was a gross contradiction, now clear to the attentive readers of these pages: a contradiction between content and form—analogous to that which we have already noted in the critique of historical materialism as a simple philosophy of history.

We will say, therefore, in conclusion, that an eclecticism of contradictory elements is the general character of this philosophy of Marx's, of which some of his disciples today are perhaps not greatly wrong in not knowing what to do. There are many fruitful ideas at its foundation, which taken separately are worthy of meditation: but isolated they do not belong, as has been proved, to Marx, nor can they therefore justify that word "Marxism," which is sought to be synonymous with a purely realistic philosophy.

It is true that the interest of science does not lie in names, and if some of the most important ideas of Hegelianism can penetrate into the mind by the allure of the name of Marx, good luck to "Marxism" too!